History of Costume

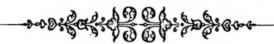

2   1660–1800

Illustrated by Faith Jaques with a commentary by Margaret Stavridi

Publishers   PLAYS, INC.   *Boston*

First American edition published
by Plays Inc. 1968
Library of Congress catalog card No. 68-8264

First published in 1967 by
Hugh Evelyn Limited
9 Fitzroy Square, London W1
© 1967 Hugh Evelyn Limited

Designed by Sheila Sherwen

The plates printed in Great Britain by
Cripplegate Printing Company Limited
and the text by
Thomas Nelson (Printers) Limited
Bound by
W. & J. Mackay & Company Limited

List of Colour Plates

Sources of Reference for the Plates

PLATE 1

a. Charles Lebrun, *The Chancellor Séguier*, 1660. Louvre.
b. Contemporary print, 1674.
c. Contemporary print, 1678.
d. Contemporary print, *c.*1680. V. & A. Museum, *17th & 18th Century Costume*, edited James Laver.

PLATE 2

a. Terborch, *Hermanna van der Cruis, c.* 1670. National Gallery.
b. Anon, *Portrait of Henry Gibbs*, 1670.
c. Terboch, *Portrait of a Gentleman*, 1665. National Gallery.
d. Anon, *Lady and Gentleman in a Garden*, Vienna, *c.* 1665. Mansell Collection.

PLATE 3

a. Caspar Netscher, *The Lace-maker*, 1664. Wallace Collection.
b. Pieter de Hooch, *Woman and her maid in a Courtyard, c.*1660. National Gallery.
c. Contemporary print, *c.*1670. V. & A.
d. Pieter de Hooch, *A Woman peeling Apples*, 1663. Wallace Collection.
e. Pieter de Hooch, *Boy bringing Pomegranates, c.*1662. Wallace collection.

PLATE 4

a, b, c, d. J. de St. Jean. Contemporary engravings. V. & A.

PLATE 5

a. J. de St. Jean. Contemporary engraving, 1694. V. & A.
b, c. Nicholas de Largillière, *James Stuart and his sister*, 1695. National Portrait Gallery.
d. J. de St. Jean. Contemporary engraving, 1693. V. & A.

PLATE 6

Tempest, *Street Cries*, 1688–1702. Mansell Collection.
a. Song-Seller b. Pot-mender c. Biscuit-seller
Objects from contemporary sources.

PLATE 7

a, b. Nicholas de Largillière, *Louis XIV and His Heirs, c.*1710. Wallace Collection.
c. Godfrey Kneller, *The Countess of Mar*, 1715.
d. Anon, *Viscount Irwin*, 1718–20.

PLATE 8

a, d. Based on statues of Charity School children, 1702–1714. Bride Lane, London.
b. Anon, *Lord John Boyle*, 1715. Orrery Papers.
c. Unidentified portrait, possibly Dutch, 1705. Mansell Collection. Urn, orange tree and macaw based on those in *James Stuart and his sister* (see plate 5).

PLATE 9

a, c. Hogarth, *The Rake's Progress*, 1735. Soane Museum.
b. François de Troy, *The Declaration of Love*, 1731. Berlin.

PLATE 10

a. Hogarth, *The Harlot's Progress*, 1732. Soane Museum.
b, c. Chardin, *Morning Toilet*, 1730.
d. Chardin, *The Nurse*, 1738. National Gallery of Washington.
Objects taken from contemporary sources.

PLATE 11

a. Gravelot, Contemporary engraving, 1744. V. & A.
b. Arthur Devis, *Miss Fenton*, 1743–5.
c. Arthur Devis, *Lady in a Park*, 1750–5. Tate Gallery.

PLATE 12

a, d, e. Hogarth, *The Graham Children*, 1742. National Gallery.
b. Hogarth, *Miss Elizabeth Hatch, c.*1740. Mansell Collection.
c. Highmore, Illustration to *Pamela, c.*1744. Fitzwilliam Museum, Cambridge.

PLATE 13

a. R. Wilson, *Prince George and Edward Duke of York, c.*1751. National Portrait Gallery.
b. Drouais, *Le Comte de Vaudeuil*, 1758. National Gallery.
c. Boucher, *La Marquise de Pompadour*, 1759. Wallace Collection.
d. Arthur Devis, *John Orde and his Family*, 1750–5. Mellon Collection.

PLATE 14

a. Gainsborough, *Countess Howe*, 1760–3. Kenwood House.
b. Gainsborough, *Viscount Kilmorey*, c.1768. Tate Gallery.
c. Nathaniel Dance (sometimes attributed to Batoni), *A Group of Englishmen in Rome*, c.1760.
d. British School, *Mrs. Cadoux*, c.1760. Tate Gallery (on loan to 10 Downing Street).

PLATE 15

a. Romney, *Jacob Morland*, c.1760. Tate Gallery.
b, c. Abbot, *Captain of the Blackheath Golf Club*, c.1780.
d. Anon, *Miss Trigger & Miss Wicket*, 1770. Mansell Collection.

PLATE 16

a, b. Moreau-le-Jeune. Contemporary prints, 1777. V. & A.
c. From Victoria & Albert Museum collection, 1777.

PLATE 17

a, b. Contemporary print, *Return from School*, by W. R. Bigg, 1780's. Mansell Collection.
c. Contemporary print, 1780. V. & A.

d. Romney, *Countess of Warwick & her children*, c.1780 Mansell Collection.
e. Romney, *Miss Charlotte Peirse*, c.1780. Mansell Collection.

PLATE 18

a, c. Contemporary engravings, 1778–80. Mansell Collection.
b. Engraving after Moreau-le-Jeune, c.1777. V. & A.

PLATE 19

a. Gainsborough, *The Morning Walk*, 1785. National Gallery.
b. Lawrence, *Angerstein and his wife*, 1790–2. Louvre.
c. Engraving after George Morland, c.1780.
d. Suit from V. & A. Collection, c.1790. Other details from Mansell Collection print, c.1790.

PLATE 20

a. Heideloff fashion plate, 1796. V. & A.
b, c. Contemporary engraving by Darcis, late 1790's. Mansell Collection.
d. Heideloff fashion plate, c.1795. Purse from London Museum, c.1790.

Preface

Ever since Adam took those figleaves and fashioned what the Geneva Bible rather generously called 'breeches', clothes have reflected the thoughts and environment of man.

Those not affected by religious taboos and the awful burden of original sin covered themselves as a protection against the elements. The caveman made his from the skin of the animal that had served him for food but as soon as the ingenious New Stone Age people had invented a way of making a thread (from grasses, the soft contents of cotton seeds and the wool of their pastoral animals) and, finally, woven strands of it together, material was made and man, positively bursting with ideas, proceeded to dye it and shape it into garments.

With more settled communities and less fight against the elements a more complicated social system arose with grades of citizens according to their job in life. The leaders of a society discovered the heaven-sent importance clothes gave to an otherwise unimpressive body, and kings lengthened the majesty of their entrance by trailing a piece of material for yards behind them or lifted their meagre stature high above their subjects by crowns or gorgeous headgear. And thus fashion was evolved.

It is possible that the clever fellows who had pushed themselves into positions of authority over tribes and – later – nations were of an all-round ability, perfectly capable of inventing outstanding garments for themselves; for the essence of fashion is the desire to be noticed and an exaggeration of the human form.

As the demand increased so the strength of the clothes-producing community grew, with dyers, spinners, weavers, tailors and embroiderers all taking their place in an important part of the social structure. Style was of necessity regionally individual owing to the type of raw material available and climatic conditions in different districts and, above all, to the inventive abilities of the leaders of each nation. There is no difficulty, now, in recognizing a picture of an ancient Egyptian in his tightly drawn muslin with the distinctive wide collar, or the Assyrian in his fringed heavy garment topped by the majestic towered head-dress.

This astonishing fund of invention has continued through the ages, reflecting the social pattern, right up to the present day when, the accepted order of society having turned topsy-turvy, instead of glorifying or distinguishing man the aim of fashion is to reduce him to one level of status, half the population of the western world being of a uniform dullness while the younger half is of a uniform commonplaceness.

Never was a period more concerned with importance and grandeur than that covered by this book, 1660–1800, especially in the early years – yet out of it grew the three dominant factors of fashion that have continued to this day, the most important being the rise and dominance of French influence and through its popularity the adoption of the Universal style whereby every well-dressed person in the countries of Europe and their colonies overseas wore clothes of an identical fashion. Except for peasants in remote districts it became impossible to identify a man by his clothes.

To be the arbiter of fashion and behaviour at this period of history meant being backed by great temporal strength, vast wealth and originality – or the cunning to project that image.

This age of monarchy possessed, in the rulers of several European countries, a remarkable number of individualists of commanding character and no small share of personal vanity, but only one with the single-mindedness of the true tycoon.

The power of Spain was already on the decline and its king, Philip IV, troubled by personal sorrow and a nagging conscience, turned pious; clinging to the black suits and high collars Velasquez had made so famous, he allowed his nation to lose the lead in fashion it had held for so long.

Charles II of England had the disadvantage of reaching the throne after a long exile, and rather favouring all things French was in no mind to compete with his cousin and neighbour.

Holland, whose star had arisen at the decline of Spain, was rich and powerful but without, as yet, a determined and decorative ruler able to sell his country's culture. So it was, despite ruinous wars with all and sundry, that Louis XIV, that practitioner in advertising born long before his time, backed by the natural genius for display and the industry of his people, managed to establish France as the arbiter of fashion for the rest of Europe. As nothing succeeds like success all were anxious to reflect the rays from the 'Sun King', and within a very short time the rulers and the well-to-do in every country of Europe wore the same costume from the curl on the periwig to the buckle on the square-toed shoe. Northern Europe having been kept sober for so long under Protestantism, the swing of the pendulum towards glamour was sudden and violent.

If in the middle years the popinjay fashions were, on serious reflection, rather cissy, Louis XIV's propensity for making an appearance in uniform with his troops on the battlefield mercifully introduced a style that hid the most shame-making part of the costume – the huge petticoat breeches – and was at the same time so comfortable and adaptable to embellishment or restraint that it has served as a basis for all male attire to this day – the fore-runner of the three-piece suit. The old military jerkin and the peasant's coat from the early years of the century, cut all in one piece with attached sleeves, now served as a model, while the doublet, which had always been covered by the jerkin if two garments were worn, now became the 'veste', or waistcoat.

The enlivening of trade with the East and a passion for things oriental coinciding with the exchange of ambassadors from Persia or Turkey gave the coat a new, exciting cachet, and the 'Persian' coat was here to stay.

It may have been noticed that it is masculine fashion that has so far been discussed, for, beautiful as women may appear in portraits by those imaginative masters of the 17th century, there had been one of those periodic recesses back to raw nature when only the male has the prerogative of display, the woman holding an inferior status in society and needing only those garments that emphasized her femininity – not her individuality or intellect.

It has been stated elsewhere that the female shoulder-line is a good indication of the dominant sex climate, and in the greater part of the 17th century it suffered depression. With the advent of more vital characters, proud or prudish, up went the shoulders and the hairstyles and more pronounced was the rear.

The period of flamboyance and display, so often in vile taste, had encouraged individuality – especially in Holland, which had suffered so cruelly under the heavy hand of political religion and was determined that thought and ideas should have expression. Out of this freedom grew a thirst for knowledge, a casting aside of the accepted theological fetters that had cramped reasoned thought, and this inquisitiveness opened up the way to the Age of Enlightenment – the enlightenment of minds to social matters, surroundings and the arts.

With the death of the King of France a weight seemed to be lifted from the manners of society.

The pompous solidity of the Baroque, which in the later years shared the dropsical malady of the old king, lightened with a more feminine, sensitive feeling, and the whole artistic world of painting, architecture, music, drama and costume burst into a picture of fragile, careless joy. Never was a period so consistent in its perfect surface appearance of proportion, colour and harmony. We now know that this was a superficial veneer and that morals were as wayward as the Rococo designs; but with licence went humour, and the veneer was so brilliant and the taste so delicate that from all the pictorial records we have of the period it is difficult not to judge it as an era of complete perfection. Honest, English Hogarth using the skill and style of his period lets the cat peep out of the bag, but even he dodges the real dirt of the physical conditions. In all the art of the 18th century there is no suspicion of stink, no muddy roads, and flea-hunting is made most engaging.

Costume played a great part in conveying this immaculate impression and as in all the other arts the proportion, grace and suitability has never been surpassed.

There is no peak above perfection in one style and without a complete break the next stage is downwards. Purity, unfortunately, palls, and with the urge to embellish and paint the lily, extravagances alter proportion and balance.

After the middle of the 18th century hairstyles leapt up to grow monstrous and overpowering. Skirts that had flowed over panniers in graceful folds were enlarged, looped up and shortened while every available inch of material was covered with decoration. Male attire kept its proportion far longer owing to the close-fitting coat and breeches, but the competition of the tall head was too great and man soon made his position as commanding as that of the woman.

The late 17th century had seen a resurgence of industry in France and England and, with the Eastern trade re-established and the home looms busily working, there was a gorgeous variety of materials to further the beauty of clothes.

The enterprising Colbert, minister to Louis XIV, in his desire to put France in the forefront of world power, enthusiastically encouraged both sources and before long a situation painfully reminiscent of our present economy arose whereby the imports strangled the home market. It was quite definitely social conditions caused by the state of the economy that precipitated the styles in costume of the last years of the century.

Every great civilization has built itself up like a pyramid with the majority supporting the few at the top. When the weight at the top becomes overpowering by too great a pressure, the base weakens and the pyramid falls. France had been in a parlous state when Louis XIV came to the throne and for many years the people groaned under cruel taxation, but with encouragement and their own inspired industry the supply was just made to meet the demands. Although humanism was entering the thoughts of the rulers of the mid-18th century they were too preoccupied to realize the simple economic fact that for those to have cake at the top enough flour has to be produced below. With an enormously increased non-food-producing, industrial community sandwiched in between, the crash was sure to come. Even with her vast agricultural resources the demand of the non-producers had been too great: the peasantry had been soaked and then drained for too long and was quite incapable of feeding itself, let alone the greedy parasites that sucked its life; the foundations cracked and the gay decorative summit crashed to the ground, the worthy with the bad. From the rubble grew a different, brave society, revolutionary in every meaning of the word as there was nothing new in the ideal – only a return to what was fondly believed to be the perfect democracy of the classical age, of which the clothes are a symbol.

The change in Britain had been less violent owing to a quite different social way of life from that of France. The edifice though shaky had never become top-heavy. Unlike the French aristocracy the English land-owner was fundamentally a man of the soil and spent a great deal of his time doing what he liked best – sporting in the country. Though dim, in many ways, he could always be got at by his people. The Gainsborough and Morland paintings are not pastoral fantasies like those of Fragonard or Moreau: the 'boudoir' pictures of the times were exclusively French.

Many years earlier the Englishman, perhaps from a more reserved nature (but it has been spitefully suggested that it was from frugality), had taken to the well-cut cloth coat except for ceremonial occasions. His Lady, when the panniers of the 'eighties were discarded, had evolved the soft-flowing, natural picture dresses so familiar from Morland's paintings. Both were more suitable for the country but could still look grand enough for town. These close-fitting male garments and high-waisted flowing gowns made a simple transition into the real classicism of the last years of the century and, strangely enough, served as a pattern on which the French, after throwing decorum to the winds, based their Empire style.

Industry and the Revolution precipitated one further great change in the costume of man. As well as the Universal style the General style now began to make its appearance. With the adoption of more sober attire the new industrial and professional middle class could now compete with the aristocracy. The first real barriers of class distinction were assailed with the introduction of the plain cloth coat, to be finally broken down by the ready-made industry in the mid-19th century.

PLATE I

Fashionable Dress

1660–1680

The effeminacy and sloppiness of male fashions in the mid-17th century must, apparently, be accounted for by the visit of an obscure Dutch (or was it German?) dignitary to Versailles just at the time when Louis XIV had projected such an image of power and glamour of himself and his people that the rest of Europe was ready to fall over itself to appear like the French.

Incredible as this may be, we have only to consider how costume had evolved over the previous years and the kind of spirit that existed in France at this time to realize how such absurdities as petticoat breeches became acceptable.

It is now generally agreed that wars, in which men of all nations were so busily engaged in the early 17th century, had brought about a proper understanding of comfort in violent activity.

There was a general loosening up from the bones and bombast of the early years: the doublet no longer fitted tightly to the body, and breeches became roomier and longer. When it was noticed that leg clothing added height and dignity to the figure and, incidentally, obscured what have ever been man's least attractive members – knobbly knees – the doublets were shortened still further to add to the illusion of greater length of leg. The busy-ness of swordplay and jumping on and off horses probably accounts for the loosened jackets and the breeches being left free at the knee.

Europe was experiencing a freedom of thought and action it had long been denied by poker-backed Spain and, as usual in history, the high spirits that had been occupied in gaining that freedom, now, at a loose end, turned to exhibitionism and petty adventure. The new freedom showed itself for a brief, exciting glimmer in England with the Cavaliers, but a hearty bible-and-sword-thumping by the Puritans held it in leash for a good many more years.

Swashbuckling was still the thing in France, where even the power of Rome sat lightly on the people, where romance dies hard and fine manners have always been of as great importance as morals. The paradoxical combination of a hard body and the silk and lace of its floppy covering is a sure indication of the reckless, devil-taunting character of the people at this time. This attitude made for ready acceptance of a new fashion, the more fantastic or provoking the better, and France, now the arbiter of taste in Europe, was able to promote any fandangle idea – and make the rest of the world like it.

The fashionable world already wore straight long breeches decorated round the waist and hems and up the sides with loops of ribbon, and festooned stockings to fill the wide tops of boots cuffed with lace. Wide baggy breeches covered by the long skirts of jerkins were still worn in the backwoods of Germany or Holland.

When the Rhinegrave of Salm made his appearance at Versailles in his probably regional costume, all dolled up for the occasion, the wild success of his visit was due, not to his presence, but to the potentialities the novelty-hungry court saw in his frilly breeches.

Rhinegraves, as they came to be called, were petticoat breeches made from many yards of material gathered on to a band round the waist. They could be cut either like divided skirts, so full that the division was invisible, or as a full petticoat frill reaching to the knees over fitting trunk-hose. From a contemporary print of a shop of the period it appears as if the petticoat was sold attached to the trunk-hose.

The French having rarely kept anything within the bounds of moderation, the fashion developed into something so monstrous that although the dashing originators could carry it off, the heavy Dutch or Germans looked most embarrassing in it, and only the most flippant Englishman subjected himself to such effeminacy, being quite ready to adopt the much more seemly fashion that followed it.

The new idea must have endeared itself quickly to Louis himself, as the skirt effect was remarkably like the lower half of a Roman Emperor and fitted in most suitably with the image he was rather heavily putting across to his people and the rest of Europe.

Pepys evidently had fun with his, remarking that it was possible to put both legs into one aperture without noticing any inconvenience.

As a further risk to composure, but very dashing, the rhinegraves were then lowered from the waist to the hips and the tops decorated in an extra frill-like effect with ribbon loops, as were the hems and sides, for as many as six or eight rows. The shirt billowed out over the top from under the doublet, now shortened to bolero length and with slit sleeves through which the shirt made another appearance. Lace frills, called cannons, fastened under the knees, filled in the undressed angle from the hem to the leg and completed the maypole effect.

Only the rich and influential could keep up with the high fashion, as the French aristocracy found to their cost when Louis XIV, having taken all power of government out of their hands, left them nothing to do but dance attendance upon himself and compete for his notice by the most extravagant appearance.

John Evelyn's sniffy remark at the sight of what he called 'a fine silken thing, drest like a maypole' gives us some idea of the general opinion in England of the new styles, but the first two figures in Plate I show what must have been quite a familiar sight in the City in the 1660's. The smart man-about-town is in the latest style, from his round wig and large turned-down collar with the fullness pleated in the front, to the wide bows on his square-toed shoes. The clerk, or superior servant, at his side illustrates how the fashion was modified into something less ludicrous for the man in the street.

Our reliable gossip columnists, Pepys and Evelyn, smugly congratulate their king and this country on launching the face-saving style that replaced or covered the most embarrassing part of the costume. Charles II was certainly the first Englishman who solemnly, and thankfully perhaps, in 1666 donned the new garment, the Persian coat, and liking it so well even took wagers that he would never alter it.

But the long coat had been seen on a few Frenchmen earlier in the decade. Louis XIV held it his duty, and thereby gathered to himself part of the glory of conquest, to appear on the battlefield with his widely engaged troops, and as by this time soldiers wore what was tantamount to uniform he appeared in an officer's loose coat, a mixture of the wide-skirted jerkin and the peasant's coat that had been worn over the past twenty or more years. A few favourite courtiers, as army officers, would have appeared thus clad at Versailles or the Louvre. With success assured and advancing years both king and court welcomed the more dignified mien the neat coat gave to the figure, but still wore it over the petticoat breeches.

The later design, called the Persian or Turkish coat from its likeness to the graceful garments seen on oriental dignitaries, differed from the military coat in that the doublet, now called a veste and bereft of its sleeves, was lengthened to form a long waistcoat which mercifully covered the breeches, and a coat of the same length took the place of the old jerkin or cloak. The whole had a loose tunic effect, but with no awkward hiatus to fill, or angle to soften, the cissy ribbons and lace frills were redundant and quickly became a laughable thing of the past.

1660 1674 *Old Billcox* 1678 *Medley* c. 1680 *Shoemaker*

Fashionable Dress

PLATE II

Domestic and Court Dress

1665–1670

It was a man's world in the 17th century, all the fun of extravagance in design or abrupt changes in style being in male costume. His was a material world of adventure, work-guilds and government, hardly an age of wisdom or spiritual activity in which man felt the need for mental stimulation from woman. Her proper function was simply to minister to his physical needs. The few women of brains and character but with no opportunity of using them to the public good immersed themselves in long correspondences or journals, furiously dashing down all the spiteful, spicy or wise ideas it would have done society the world of good to hear but which they had no power to express publicly. The miserably few adventurous ones, such as Christina, Queen of Sweden, or the Grande Mademoiselle, either became laughing-stocks or succumbed to male expediency.

The nice Dutch groups show a certain equality of the sexes, with the laughing girls and entertaining men, but there is a self-conscious glumness about English and even French portraits, with the male figure always in the position of importance.

This lack of initiative is very obvious in women's clothes up to the end of the century when a few strong-minded souls managed, by their persistence and example, to impress upon fashion a little more personality.

Female dress hardly altered over fifty years except for the neck or waist line going up or down according to the moral climate of the time.

After the stiff padded skirts and hard boned bodices with round ruffs or upturned lace collars went out of fashion, a beautiful simple line prevailed with a straight, higher waist and softly gathered skirts. The high lace collar, the Medici, now turned down over a square *décolletage*, could either be rolled back from the opening or worn fastened under the chin to cover the neck and shoulders. The wide breadth of the collar made an unbroken line from the neck to the sleeve and the female shoulder-line took the downward slope so illustrative of her character in the 17th century.

The only variation in the style came when women turned up their skirts and fastened them on the hips to give a pannier effect and show different-coloured petticoats. In the more conservative countries, such as Holland, this style lasted well on into the century.

The bodice was the first to show a real change about 1660, when the front was stiffened anew and carried lower than the waist into a sharp point. The diverging front seams were carried up from the point over the edge of the shoulders in a wide triangle which began to be decorated with graduated-size bows, after the male beribboned style. Later, with braid or embroidery up the seams, it gave the impression of a separate stomacher. The decoration down the front of the bodice was sometimes continued down the middle of the skirt and no doubt suggested the next evolution – the open-fronted dress over a contrasting-coloured petticoat.

The continued popularity of the collar was due to the influence of Holland which, for a short time through wealth and political power (to say nothing of its numerous great painters who could project a gorgeous image of its culture), took the lead in setting the fashion after the power of Spain waned and the rest of Europe remained in the doldrums.

The *décolletage* is the real clue to the changed spirit of the times. The respectable lady – nurse or even Grandmama – in our Plate II wears the simple yet becoming dress of every middle-class woman during the middle and later years of the 17th century and clings to the conservative collar which veils the square-cut opening of her dress and, clinging to the shoulders and upper arm, illustrates the typical silhouette of the period.

Necklines had now become practically horizontal with even the shoulder showing and the really outstanding beauties of the time did nothing to prevent their ample bosoms from swelling over the top.

There were Mrs Grundys even at the jovial court of Charles II or the equally lax Versailles, such as the Duchess of Orleans ('Liselotte' of the prodigious journals) who veiled her ample shoulders in what was to be known as a 'palatine', after her first title, in the hope that her example would be followed by the lesser ladies of the court. It is from her effort that we get the delightful word 'tippet', which John Evelyn describes as the 'winter palatine', made from sable tails.

The grand lady on the right of the picture, though Dutch, now wears the Universal style and would be equally fashionable in France or England, but follows the more decorous example of the plump Duchess by wearing a thin gauze scarf pulled in, in the shape of a collar, over her wide, open neckline.

What the dress lacked in complication was made up for in the extravagant sleeves, often put into the shoulder-line with cartridge pleats to make the stiff satin stand out in a short rounded curve through which the chemise or under-sleeve billowed out in puffs and lace frills to be caught in with ribbons and bows.

With the wide shape given by the horizontal neckline, the full sleeves and the rounded skirt, the hairstyle was kept suitably low and full over the ears. Parted in the middle with tiny tendrils on the temples, the hair gradually widened at the sides, over wire frames, while one or two curls were allowed to descend as love locks on to the shoulders.

Small caps were worn by older women and, for out-of-doors, heads were covered by a hood-like shawl, often of black lace, which repeated the shawl or stole pulled tightly round the body to follow the sloping line of the shoulders.

The complacent gentleman in the centre of his family is the clearest example we have of the fashion of the 1660's at its most extreme but without the French panache. The Dutch could afford the latest fashion but were slow to change, as we see from the high-crowned hat that had become *démodé* in England and France. Nevertheless, the style of dress must have continued well into the 1670's for the less up-to-the-minute population, as can be seen from engravings, both Dutch and French,

of the ordinary townsfolk. Children were grown-ups in miniature, the noble child being as stiffened with bones and backboards as the fashion demanded. The luckier lower classes, though still wearing the exact shape of their elders, were allowed a little more elbow room and breathing space. Boys up to the age of six still wore female skirts and, except when wearing a man's befeathered beaver, are quite indistinguishable from their sisters.

England apparently suffered from a patch of blind snobbery until the 18th century, ignoring in painting anyone or anything less than a Lord or his possessions. The Dutch, Flemish and even French, fortunately for posterity, enjoyed painting the everyday things, the towns and the people who lived and worked in them, and without the camera they have left a pretty good impression of the life of the times.

c. 1668 1670 1665 c. 1665

Domestic and Court Dress

PLATE III

Domestic Dress

1660–1670

Before the new French styles became generally popular, rich Holland filled the gap left by waning Spanish influence on costume and manners.

East Indian trade, which necessitated a strong navy and a vast merchant marine, had brought the Dutch to a peak of political and economic power in the mid-17th century. The nature of their religion and the democracy of their social system, due to the purse strings being held by the merchant class, touched a sympathetic chord in the make-up of the people of Northern Europe. This was particularly so in England where the mainly dissenting merchant and professional families were beginning to form a large, well-to-do middle class to whom the comfortable and sober dress of the solid-looking people of the Netherlands was most acceptable.

Though statistics show that the peasant and working classes far outnumbered the aristocracy and landed gentry in England at this time, their life seems to have had no interest for the native painters, and except for woodcuts and primitive engravings we have few records of the modes and manners of the ordinary people. True, we also lacked the painters. The Dutch and Flemish, on the other hand, were completely satisfied with themselves, a fact that their many inspired artists, such as Netscher or Ter Borch, spared no time or canvas to tell the rest of Europe. Even the French, with the Le Nain family, left us an image of every aspect of non-U daily life.

The Dutch houses of this period give us a very favourable impression of an unostentatious but comfortable family background, with the very pictures that now tell us so much about them on the walls, and beautiful rugs and china that bear witness to the successful Eastern trade.

London, after the fire, must have looked rather like the pictures by de Hooch with the new red brick houses replacing the picturesque but cramped black-and-white timbered buildings that had blazed so furiously from Pudding Lane to Pie Corner, and as our ties with Holland were very close during the 17th century there must have been a great deal in common between the lands of the Orange and the Rose.

The way of life of the Dutch burghers appears to have been dignified and easy-going, with a lot of good eating and drinking and fun and games in the kitchen and taverns. Religious observance was evidently hardly repressive, with children playing tag round the columns in church which the dogs used for other purposes.

Fine materials made their rich clothes, and their commodious cupboards were full of beautiful embroidered linen which was all produced either in the house or in some peasant's cottage. The big estates in England had been self-supporting since Tudor times with their carpenters, blacksmiths, farmers and dairy workers to see to their external and physical needs while the women of the house busied themselves with the complicated preparation of wool or flax for the making of material for their own clothes and the household linen.

In those pensionless, welfare-stateless days families, from pride, had to look after less fortunate members, and the extra hands of maiden aunts, cousins and widowed in-laws were even welcomed to man the spinning wheels and embroidery frames that were not merely, as is generally supposed, the means of passing otherwise tedious hours but the very necessary part of the household economy that is now provided for us commercially.

The lace collars, ribbons and embroidery represented in the thousands of portraits and genre pictures of this period would add up to hundreds of miles of beautiful handwork – a staggering realization to those who have seen such inferior copies churned out at the pressure of a button. All the lace and embroidery was produced at this stage in the villages by peasant women, under the tutelage, certainly in France, of the nuns of the convents which had many great ladies retreating from a strenuous life at court or in society among their members. It was not only the rich or smart who wore these refinements; the peasant girl would use the same patterns for her pretty bonnet or wedding gown, a fact that can be proved by the lovely national costumes that have been handed down as heirlooms and are still worn in European countries on fête days.

When high fashion borrowed some of the eccentricities or sensible lines of peasant clothes, as already pointed out, there was a gradual linking of styles by which the wide disparity of shape between the rich and fashionable and the workaday world was less apparent. The often rich but untitled merchant class were even daring to compete with the nobility, and the numerous 'sumptuary laws', forbidding the wearing of this collar or that material, ribbons or lace and a hundred and one petty items, show us how doggedly, but with decreasing success, the aristocracy clung to the privilege of distinction by dress.

The Dutch style of woman's dress shows very clearly the basic shape of the mid-17th century costume which remained the same in silhouette no matter in what material or however overloaded with trimming. To give the desired slope to the shoulders the front panel of the bodice was carried wide and low over the top of the arm to meet the back piece in a seam low on the shoulder-blade. The full sleeves were gathered in cartridge pleats, low on the shoulder-line and again into a wide cuff from which the chemise peeped in ruffles or a second cuff.

The wide lace or lawn collar, covering or filling in the *décolletage*, is almost a symbol of the 17th century except in the useful little garment that the burgher's good wife seems to have launched at this time but which was to become so important all through the following century – the *matinée*.

These little coats or overblouses without any stiffening and hardly fitting to the figure must have been a boon to the plump and easy-going woman who otherwise had to support the torture of the whalebone, horsehair and lacing of the full dress bodice. It is not to be wondered at that so many received visits in bed or in their dressing rooms – a very rare incidence of comfort overcoming fashion. Modest caps covered the little bun of hair drawn up at the back of the head and the side curls that, on party occasions, sprang out wide over the ears.

Harking back to those jolly Dutch pictures, life was gay, we are happy to note, for the young at this time in spite of their miniature grown-up clothes. Little caps topped neat heads and the boys wore full-skirted breeches, like the men, but that didn't stop them climbing trees, picking apples or bird-nesting. Little girls, even in leading-strings, or reins, which were fastened to their shoulders, could gird up their kirtles and play a pretty stroke of golf, even, apparently, in the house!

1664   c. 1660   1670   1663   c. 1662

Domestic Dress

PLATE IV

Fashionable French Dress

1686–1694

The extravagance and development of high fashion in the late 17th century was most probably due to the foxy manoeuvre of Louis XIV in keeping the affairs of state in his own capable hands and his wretched nobles in a perpetual state of anxiety and subjection. The bullying he had received in early years, from his mother and wily statesmen, enlightened his acute mind to the idea that a sovereign he must be, in every sense of the word.

His mistrust for his nobles only equalled his distaste for the rabble, who had dared to force their way into his room when he was a child, optimistically hopeful that their young king would be interested in their cause. To remove his august presence as far as possible from a repetition of this irritation and his nobles from the politically stimulating atmosphere of Paris, he caused Versailles to be built and set up a court so exacting in ritual and aimless in intention that over-dressing to catch the king's eye was the only occupation left to those dogged enough to stand the strain.

Court life became a masque of fashion with the competing courtiers as definitely unpaid extras. It says much for the personality and will of Louis XIV that such a large group of Frenchmen seriously submitted for so long to standing about for hours, watching the king eat, dress, play cards or, as a little relief, take the leading part in a masque dressed like an overblown ballerina, all for the chance of hearing their names on the king's lips or the honour of handing the royal bed-socks. The few less dim-witted sought relief in fighting, an activity he very often allowed since enthusiastic officers were always useful and also expendable.

The outward appearance of the court at Versailles was indeed an enviable marvel. With the ostentatious background of the palace, its furnishings and gardens executed with the utmost attention to detail, the humans were expected to add the final touch of gorgeous ornamentation, and as the French have never been at a loss in the matter of decoration the court did their sovereign proudly. As in all advertising, the expense

was enormous; it was also another clever method whereby the king ensured that his nobles' wealth was not used to his own danger. The fact that this crippled the vast estates of France – and therefore, eventually, the national economy – was a matter that did not immediately concern him.

In the centre of all the court's splendour shone Louis himself, and although it is said that he never descended to the level of creating styles he was vain and fashion-conscious and on him rested the power of launching the latest ideas.

Envy and admiration, certainly, caused the popularity of French fashions abroad, but it must be noted that where adoption was a trifle laggard Louis took firm measures to see that few pockets of resistance were left, as in the case of the occupation of Strasbourg in 1681, when the inhabitants were ordered to assume French costume within four months.

It was through Louis XIV that the coat, for general and civil wear, came into being and was altered and embellished right through to the 18th century and on till today. To keep this fashion exclusive at first and therefore tempting, the king established a royal warrant to wear embroidered, fitted coats, the 'justaucorps à brevet', reserving to himself and a few favourite courtiers the right to wear them.

The coat started as a long loose garment, only slightly fitted to the figure, covering the wide gathered breeches. By 1680 rhinegraves and knee frills were démodé and fitted breeches took their place, closed by buttons, garters or a buckled strap, or covered by long hose rolled over the knee. By the 1680's coats became knee-length and increasingly fitted at the waist, with the back seams of the skirts unsewn so that the stiffened and pleated flaps lapped over each other. Coats were generally left unbuttoned to show the equally decorated veste, or long waistcoat, which was closed up to the cravat. As the century advanced even vestes were left open to receive the ends of the lacy neck-cloth. Pockets, which had opened vertically or diagonally on the coat skirts, were then set horizontally low on the front panels and decorated with braid and buttons to match the rest of the coat. Sleeves became narrower and, by a decree of Louis XIV in 1665, lost the slit through which the under-shirt had billowed. Wide cuffs turned back to the elbow with extravagant trimming made up in importance for the loss of decoration in the upper sleeve. There were no collars, as the great wigs covered the neck to the shoulders and often beyond, but the fronts could be turned back like lapels to show a coloured lining.

The cravat evolved from the 'falling-bands' or collars of the mid-17th century which, narrowed at the back, fell in a square bib under the chin. This same lace or lawn was lengthened and the ends turned one over the other to form a neck-cloth. Before the frilly period faded, in the 1680's, ribbons round the neck ended in pussy bows, sticking out on either side from under the cravat ends. These grew more important as the century aged and could be tucked into the breeches, tossed over the shoulder or festooned and pulled through a buttonhole of the coat as shown in our fashion of 1693. This also shows how, in warm weather, the veste could be daringly discarded and the floppy white shirt displayed down to the waist.

Boots were out of fashion by 1660 and square-toed shoes took their place, with rosettes or wide bows over the high front. The present to the French king, by the designer and shoemaker of Bordeaux, of a special line of footwear, comprising high red heels and bows spanning sixteen inches across the instep, so enchanted the recipient that he vowed he would wear no other shape, and in the succeeding years men of fashion tottered in ankle shoes with three-inch heels and bows that impeded the step.

The outstanding symbol of the period was, of course, the periwig, that exaggeration of the previously fashionable long natural hair.

Louis XIV clung to his own fine locks until he became prematurely bald in 1673 and thereafter encouraged the wigmakers to heights of extreme fantasy. Having started smoothly in a rounded shape reaching to the shoulders the front hair was then teased into hornlike curls in the general uplifting and narrowing of the lines of dress in the 1690's. As habits of cleanliness were mainly ignored, the condition of these head pieces is something one would rather not dwell upon. Pepys did draw the line at purchasing a new one round about 1665, suspecting, probably quite rightly, that the bodies of plague victims would have yielded a fine supply of real hair. As wigs grew higher, crowns of hats were lowered to perch on top and the wavy brims were bent inwards, at first in one place, then three, to make the three-cornered hat so popular in the 18th century. Plumes that had rioted on top of the crown were then placed round the inside of the edge of the brim.

With exquisite efficiency the French produced fashion-plates to further the image of their splendour. These fine engraved plates, purporting to be of distinguished personages, throw a light on more than the details of dress. The lavish use of fur and the huge muffs are a reflection of the excessively hard winters that gripped Europe during the last two decades of the 17th century.

1694   1693   Dorimont   1686   Sir Fopling Flutter   1693

Fashionable French Dress

PLATE V

Women's and Children's Dress

1693–1695

Speaking of the behaviour of the 17th century, Macaulay says that the effect of licentiousness was the moral and intellectual degradation of woman. Brains and character are certainly not the attributes that Lely sought to convey in his rows of portraits of royal favourites, or that can be found in the innumerable pictures of the ladies of Versailles, they are so nearly identical, in the soft erotic drapery of the mid-17th century, that one must conclude that popular fancy demanded something dumb, blonde or otherwise, that could be replaced by an exact duplicate when the original showed signs of wear.

The monotonous regularity with which succeeding favourites retired into convents, with the acid comment that the strict Carmelite rules would be a haven of peace after the humiliation and suffering of their previous existence, should have been a pointer to the eager queue of aspirants ready to step into their shoes, but it was many years before the line of clothes showed that a changed spirit towards woman was abroad.

It is satisfying to record that a rare incidence of virtue and integrity had its reward, on this earth, not in Puritanical oppression but in a quiet example that was so strong that the whole of woman's world was to feel and show the effect. Too little credit has been paid to the dignified, widowed woman who, entering court circles as the governess of the illegitimate children of Louis XIV, made herself so indispensible to the king, for qualities far removed from physical attraction, that he finally married her in 1684.

Madame de Maintenon had none of the attributes of a contemporary court favourite but she had tact and intelligence and a background of informed culture from her association with leading thinkers of the day while married to her first husband, the poet-dramatist, Paul Scarron. She was, moreover, an early champion of better education for women. Louis XIV was only forty-six at the time of his second marriage and still a fine figure of a man, but by the miracle of a sympathetic companionship with a sensible woman he became a pattern of domestic respectability and the whole tone of court life was raised. With less skylarking at Versailles the ever imitative courts of Europe fell into step and the higher status of women was soon apparent.

This being a history and not a tract it is not suggested that the new image of woman was more beautiful than in the lush, licentious days, but that with more self-respect her whole appearance showed individuality and character and a very much more interesting line in clothes.

Looseness of behaviour had an echo in the shoulder-slipping, chemise-showing styles of the 1660's, '70's and '80's, but with the coming of the 1690's a general uplift made its appearance. Where the silhouette had been wide and full it now narrowed, and head-dresses heightened to add further dignity. Bodices were the first to undergo a change, the wide front pieces being carried up straight over the shoulder, filling in the rounded neckline of the earlier fashion. With modesty as the key-note the neck was also more concealed, often by a cravat, tied in the manner of the men's 'steinkirk' which took its name from the battle at which the victorious French were so eager to engage that the fashionable General had no time to finish dressing and hastily knotted his cravat and threaded the ends through his buttonhole – thus creating a new fashion.

Overdresses – a bodice and gored skirt open right down the front and caught back in a bustle over a contrasting petticoat – revealed an embroidered stomacher with a straight top that squared off the *décolletage*.

The complement of the male periwig in pinpointing the period is the peculiar feminine head-dress. This arose from the hair being narrowed over the ears while the front was raised in twin peaks with tiny curls on either side of the forehead. As the hair rose, little caps that had perched on the back of the head had their frills widened in front and tipped up to frame the high curls over the forehead. With the front frills wired to stand upright and the sides lengthened into lappets over the shoulder, or tied under the chin, the confection was called the 'commode', or tower. The slightly later version, of a high-standing fan of pleated lace, got its name, we are told, from the attractive Duchesse de Fontange who, having lost her hat while hunting, tied up her wayward front curls with her lace garter. When the fashion of the top-knot of lace evolved several years later (after the lady had succumbed to a frequent malady of court favourites – poison), her appearance was remembered and the erection dubbed *'fontange'*. With a crest on top, and a train and bustle behind, women now had an air of the divine assurance of the peacock.

Women protected themselves against the icy winters with the same chic as the men; fashion-plates show such rich items as entire overdresses of ermine, muffs and the sensible house wraps that were beginning to make their appearance as a revolt against the stiffness of formal dress. These followed the same lines as an overdress but were looser, lined for winter, and had long comfortable sleeves, albeit braided and decorated in the overpowering manner of the late 17th century.

Patches, those blemish-hiders of an earlier part of the century, became extremely fashionable in the later part, but with a slightly different emphasis, being placed near, and to point to, a particularly attractive feature. Stars and crescent moons were common but the really provocative had much fun with cupids and even a coach and pair.

Masks were borrowed from Italy to liven up state balls where, the participants being so well known to each other, the proceedings were apt to be tedious. They were even countenanced for ladies wishing to walk incognito in the streets.

The lot of noble children was as confining and straight-laced as their grown-up clothes. At a very early age a separate establishment was provided for them under the supervision of a governess, herself a very grand lady, usually a duchess in the case of royal children.

Their constriction is very apparent in the baby leading-strings built-in to the little princess's dress, although a tall *'fontange'* rises on her head and her ornate apron matches the rich stiffened stomacher.

The little prince displays the waisted, pleat-skirted coat of 1695, opened to the waist button in a sophisticated, adult manner to show a glimpse of the metal-studded brocade of the waistcoat which, in this case, is sleeved, as can be seen from the turned-back band over the deep coat cuff. The simple trimming of gold braid and buttons foreshadows the more restrained style of the next century but the wide bows under the cravat are of an earlier fashion, probably still used to give greater importance to a small boy's neck. The hat is of the latest fancy with brim cocked into a true tricorne edged with a narrow feather trimming, while his shoes sport the new square buckle, in place of the wide bows, and natty turned-over tops to match the high red heels.

1694   1695   1695   1693

Women's and Children's Dress

PLATE VI

Street Vendors

1688-1702

Changes of fashion have to be recorded at the date when there is a visible alteration in shape seen in dated portraits or pictures. Until the age of cheap ready-to-wear in the late 19th century these changes were only to be seen on those who wished to be conspicuous and had the leisure and money to wear and pay for them. What the rest of the world looked like was quite another matter – probably five years or more behind the times. Even now, the crowds shopping in Oxford Street look somehow different from the dummies in the windows. Luckily for the historian there are pictorial records other than the portraits of the rich or pictures of fashionable occasions.

While the French court continued to parade the increasingly overloaded high fashion at Versailles and the English court slowly sank into a heavy torpor under its overweight and disinterested sovereigns, the life of the people quickened perceptibly.

To start with, there were many more of them, in spite of the plague, wasting-fever and drink. Paris and London had grown into large towns, especially the latter through its importance as the world's busiest port and trading centre. The essential difference between the two capitals, which had such dire consequences for the French nobility ninety years later, was that where Paris produced for its ornamental upper class, isolated and spend-thrift at Versailles, London was the centre of a smart, intellectual and business life where all classes rubbed shoulders together and benefited from the exchange. The rich London merchants still lived near their warehouses or over their shops, but as the menace of coal smoke grew they built themselves smart villas in the hamlets of Clapham, Hampstead or Chelsea in the first steps towards the great suburbia of the 19th century.

London was not only the greatest port in the world, where she greedily pulled in the commodities from the east, west and Africa to be processed and sold all over the country : she had become a truly cosmopolitan centre of financial dealings necessary to the running of overseas commerce, in which she was most efficiently assisted by the Jewish settlement of business-men who had been admitted into the country during the Commonwealth. Above all, the metropolis was a manufacturing centre. London, like a great fat spider, welcomed all and sundry and grew fatter on the efforts of the tip-top craftsmen from other countries who sought refuge from religious persecution and unemployment. The Huguenots' Spitalfields silks and brocades, the leather workers and jewellers all added to the commodities that could be consumed internally or exported.

With plenty of work for plenty of labour the Englishman would seem to have been sitting pretty when Queen Anne creakily ascended the throne. In fact a great many were, but with the growing population of town dwellers the big cities began to fester into slums which, like the poor, are with us still. The Great Fire had not, unfortunately, destroyed the worst over-crowded part of the City to the east which, consequently, had not been rebuilt. Even in the west, where smart new buildings were being erected for the well-to-do, pockets of the old, crowded, insanitary housing still remained and into these cheap quarters swarmed the people of no property, the casual labour and the downright vicious. Left to themselves with neither medical aid, police nor religious uplift they gradually coagulated into the hearty, tough community that has borne the brunt of keeping the wheel of the great city turning to this day. These were no ghettos: the people sallied forth to load the ships, supply and serve the great markets and titillate the rich while emptying their pockets. They also became the suppliers of the everyday needs of the large middle class and their own community.

The famous markets had their licensed pitches but did not necessarily operate every day. The shops were rather grand affairs catering mainly for the rich, with quite often the younger sons of country gentry as apprentice assistants hoping to make fortunes in their turn, the English having rarely been too snobbish to engage in retail commerce – as Napoleon so rudely pointed out a century later.

The needs of the humbler household had to be supplied by the street vendor who fetched the fish from Billingsgate, the coal from Thames barges and the fruit and vegetables from the market gardens of Battersea, or would mend your chairs, pots and pans or sweep your chimney. The faint echo of their cries, from the last strawberry-man, is apt to produce a nostalgic pang in these days of self-service, no delivery and no repairs.

That this was a large and picturesque community we see from the popular contemporary prints of the Cries of London, from which we also see that their appearance altered very slightly, as the same pictures were issued at regular intervals over a period of years. Not for them the eccentricities of the latest style; their costume had a very independent and individual flavour which, in the pictures at least, they wore with a certain panache. But it is curious to note that when at last the high fashion changed it resembled very closely the dress of the peasant or working woman of the late 17th century. Hats are a case in point: they could hardly have been worn over a high bonnet or 'fontange' but we see them on the song-sellers and lavender-girls of William the III's London. It is quite probable that, much as the Cockney woman in living memory wore her husband's cloth cap, her ancestor flaunted the man's wide-brimmed felt over a loose kerchief tied under her chin. A few years later the grand lady looked very much the same with a fine straw or silk-covered hat tied over her tiny bonnet.

The London Criers wore laced bodices, with elbow sleeves showing the frilled chemise under the cuffs, and long straight aprons, much more in the manner of the 1730's than the short square aprons of fashionable wear in 1700. Skirts were full and gathered at the waist, preparing the way for the panniers of the next fashion, and were sensibly short to show the type of shoe that had been worn for thirty years, with the high front, square toe and wide bow.

The old dissenter streak in the people of London died hard, as we see from the kerchief round the neck of the biscuit-woman in the manner of a Puritan collar, and even her bodice sports the jerkin shoulder. The men who sold coal or fish, or mended pans, had an equally typical air. They, too, donned long coats, if they were lucky enough to get reach-me-downs from a colleague who also cried his wares, wearing as many as six hats, one on top of another, on his head. As often as not their top covering was the jerkin of the country man or soldier, but their breeches were close-fitting, and all wore the slouch hats with the pliable brims which, cocked this way or that, seem to typify Defoe's London.

Song-seller

Orange Woman

Pot-mender

Biscuit-seller

Street Vendors 1688–1702

PLATE VII

Court and Country Dress

1710–1719

The hold over Europe of French culture was as strong as ever when the 18th century began, but more from habit than from inspiration. The taste and disposition of the ageing Maintenon, her influence over the king, and his own lack of interest for any more experiment, had brought the arts to a state of stagnation, and costume, in particular, was in the doldrums for nearly thirty years.

Baroque art had blown itself out to its fullest extent and clothes, likewise, had no room for another swag, festoon or tassel. The next step could only be towards a complete change, but while the autocrat Louis XIV still held control, that was completely out of the question.

The stiff-backed, tedious code of etiquette brought to perfection by Louis himself, as a revulsion from the brutal manners of his youth, when added to a new primness of moral behaviour, had a strong reflection in the armour-plated, tight-laced dresses of the women. The male withdrew so impersonally into his outer shell that only the most remarkable features are recognizable in portraits, peeping out of the jungle of periwig, and the figures inside the heavily reinforced, beskirted coats might just as well be dummies.

The only concession to change in women's dress was in a little softness, with the skirt fullness gathered into the waist instead of being gored, which had given it a triangular shape from the long tight bodice.

It is said that even Louis had shown his weariness on several occasions for the 'fontange,' as the head-dress had grown to monstrous heights with so much metal-work to keep the frills erect that a French wit had suggested that hairdressers should also be blacksmiths! The reaction of the court beauties was to dip the fan-shaped frills almost horizontally, and unbecomingly, before the fashion disappeared through (and it is difficult to believe) the appearance of an English duchess at the court of Versailles, wearing her hair parted in the middle and softly dressed close to her head. The king was so impressed that his admiration and caustic

comment in regard to the head-dresses of his own ladies furled their sails overnight. A style does not necessarily originate in the country that makes it the vogue for general wear, nor need the originator be recognized as fashionable. English women have seldom been credited with chic but there have always been a few characters of beauty and independence who wore what they liked with great distinction.

It is in this rigid period, strangely enough, when the general status of woman was at a low ebb, that we see the first faint effort to exert her rights and individuality which had such a distinct bearing on her appearance.

The tactics employed were as varied as the complicated psychological urge that brought them into being. To achieve equal rights with man, mentally and materially, without losing the delight of a special physical relationship, is a knotty problem that has still to be worked out satisfactorily. The French method in woman's first attempts to assert her identity, in the late 17th century, was to prove equality of intellect, resulting in the famous Salons where already established women of fashion entertained the thinkers of the day. Many words and much scandal were exchanged but the effort had no effect whatsoever on woman's appearance as fascination was the bait and the movement never left the drawing-rooms.

A more primitive gambit was to imitate the male, and even this had a dual means of expression: as a provocation, by wearing men's attire to accentuate female characteristics and frailty, or by finding some means to equal his physical prowess. Both urges had some satisfaction in a very restricted field – in riding.

As the means of asserting independence, over many centuries, the symbol of woman's emancipation should really be the horse. Women have always ridden; even the ancient Greeks permitted them to race, clad as lightly as the men, but after those more broad-minded days a special costume for the exercise seems to have escaped the interest of designers. A farthingale was not the most suitable or elegant of costumes for sitting on a horse.

When male clothes became increasingly feminine in the mid-17th century, the golden opportunity of levelling the appearance of the sexes was not missed by the brighter elements in the courts of either France or England. Very provocative was Madame de Montespan's show-stopping turn-out for one of the equestrian entertainments at Versailles which was matched, in intention, by that of Frances Stewart (of the Britannia-on-the-penny fame) at the court of Charles II. Her military doublet, periwig and feathered hat undoubtedly had the right effect in some quarters, though Samuel Pepys plaintively recorded that 'at no point could the wearer be taken for a woman'!

The other variation on the same theme brought into being the 'horsey woman'. Mounted, she could compete physically with man (and look very dashing, withal) and, from the time we first get a glimpse of her in the plays of Congreve, we follow her, booted and whip-flicking through two centuries, until as the New Woman she changed her steed for the bicycle. In the early 18th century her riding costume was identical with male attire, with the exception of the long, wide skirt to the habit. The coat, open to show the laced waistcoat, and the carelessly tied 'steinkirk' topped by a full periwig, could all have been made for a man, and it is interesting to note that the coat pockets are still vertically placed, for easier use while seated on a horse.

It was not until the 1720's that much change took place in men's costume. Coats had tended to become plainer, with only braid and buttons outlining the edges and pockets, leaving to the waistcoats all the richness of brocade and embroideries.

It was about this time, too, that the Englishman began to wear more extensively the type of suit that was to become the pattern for men's wear eighty years later, made from what had been England's greatest economic asset over many centuries – fine woollen cloth. This was indeed an innovation since coat, waistcoat and breeches could all be made of the same material and with the substitution of riding boots for the buckled shoes could be worn for various occasions with fine effect. Fundamentally of a sober nature and enjoying an outdoor life, the Englishman had always inclined to less flamboyant clothes and, from now on, silks, satins and embroidery were worn only by fops and for formal occasions. The periwig gradually became less engulfing, hardly reaching to the shoulders, with the back hair tied with a ribbon bow or caught up into a bag.

A grey head, showing age and experience, was much in favour at the dawn of the Age of Wisdom. For those who had acquired the latter but had lost the means of showing them, wigs sprinkled with rice powder gave back that air of distinction. So becoming was the fashion found to be that, before long, young and old were busily powdering, in a vogue that lasted well into the century.

c. 1710 *Lady Woodvill*   c. 1710 *Young Bellair*   1715   c. 1719 *Old Bellair*

Court and Country Dress

PLATE VIII

Children's Dress

1705–1715

Battered by mass communication on the subject of education, and conscience-stricken on the question of equal opportunity for all, the modern individual might be excused for thinking that the argument had been a burning preoccupation of the British from way back in time. It is with surprise and perhaps a little envy that we learn that only two hundred and fifty years ago the great mass of the population was blissfully ignorant of the nightmare of 11-plus and O-levels.

Education had been undertaken by the Church until the Reformation and had embraced all of the community likely to benefit. When the monks were relieved of their lands and responsibilities there was little to fill the gap, as the schools that had been endowed by private persons, guilds or societies were not numerous enough to cover the wide field that the monastic institutions had done.

In spite of a little more concern on the subject and a hurried building and opening of grammar schools in the time of Edward VI and Queen Elizabeth, the available education was still only open to the wealthy or to the very clever poor boy thought to be of potential use to the community, who was thus raised out of his station. The 18th century has been called the Age of Enlightenment due to the enormous strides in learning, philosophy, and the humanities that developed later in the century, but at its dawn the candle had hardly begun to flicker.

Kings were still despotic rulers, intent only on their own diversions; governments ruled for the benefit of their sovereigns and the prestige of their country, and the common man was tolerated only to minister to those of higher degree.

Though damped down, the fire of democracy had never really died in England after the Commonwealth. We had had our revolution, put the king in his place, and the people had had a good innings at running the country. Dismal business as it proved to be, the principles of commonwealth and righteous living had survived the jollification of the Restoration and remained in the hard core of Dissenters who formed a great part of the middle class and working population.

These worthies, debarred from entrance to universities and most schools by the triumphant Church of England, had diligently set to work to create their own places of education and, to the concern of the establishment, made an excellent job of it.

The Anglican Church, alerted to the danger of an educated opposition, hastened to establish places of learning of their own and by the end of the reign of Queen Anne the Charity Schools for the Poor were in operation all over the country.

The curriculum was rather restricted – to reading, writing and strongly-emphasized religious teaching. Competition with the dissenters was not the only spur to the spreading of general education. Nor was pure philanthropy. The merits of an early indoctrination in accepted behaviour and in the habit of subordination in the lower classes, which is the strongest safeguard against rebellion and social upheaval, were discoveries made two centuries before the Nazi regime.

The brighter side of the enterprise was the democratic manner in which it was put into practice by enlisting the co-operation of local interest from the middle class and workers themselves, who were coerced into subscribing towards expenses and taking a hand in the control of the schools.

Far removed as general education may seem from our subject, in reality it had an enormous bearing on the appearance of the youth of this country. Dirty little ragamuffins would hardly have been a good advertisement for the worthy enterprise and one can imagine the concern that occupied school committees on the important matter of clothing. Was it good taste, fortuitous chance, or a cheap and easily come-by dye from the indigo vats of the East India Company, that made them choose the becoming-to-all blue?

Some of the endowed schools had their distinctive uniform. Those formed in Tudor days wore the economically designed gown and doublet, all in one piece, that we know so well from the boys of Christ's Hospital.

There was nothing of fancy dress about the choice of costume for the Charity Schools; it was quite up-to-date and, at the time, would have been envied rather than disparaged by those less fortunate than the wearers. The modern theory of free-for-all had yet to come. One still had to be 'deserving'.

The shape chosen for the girls followed the line of normal wear, with a full skirt, laced bodice and short, cuffed sleeves. A hint of the religious nature of the organization crept into the wide white collar but the bonnet had frills gathered and lifted in front, to match fashionable headgear. The boys' smart cloth coats were miniatures of those worn by the majority of men in England at the time – slightly waisted, large-cuffed and trimmed with handsome buttons. Coat skirts were knee-length and shaped, and it can be noticed that the breeches now cover the knees, the waistcoat is shorter and the pockets higher, in the style that became the mode for many years.

The cost of clothing a deserving girl in 1708 was ten shillings and threepence, while the authorities got off more lightly with the boys at nine shillings and twopence. Luckily for the school budget, attendance did not cover many years and, no doubt, these serviceable garments were handed down to smaller brothers and sisters.

With 25,000 children attending Charity Schools and as many the educational institutions of the dissenters, the higher standard of social well-being and cleanliness in the young must have been quite noticeable.

Uniform was only enforced in the endowed schools, as clothes had to be provided for the poor pupil by the authorities. Snobbery had not yet made it seem essential that a boy should spend his early years exclusively in the company of others of his own class, and a thrifty squire's son could occupy the place originally intended for the deserving poor boy, side by side with the sons of local trades-people. Sober clothes were favoured, even at the great Public Schools where the fees, at £26 a year, were as modest as the standard of education offered. It was at the Gentlemen's Academies, just opening, that one could really make a splash, wearing the latest cut in coats of fine cloth, the doggy neckwear of the grown-up and a hair-do that the modern young man might envy.

No simpler clothing than that of a grown woman was thought necessary for the poor little rich girl whose educational outlook was indeed bleak. Her mother's knee was deemed a more suitable place of instruction than a school desk, owing to a strongly held theory that there was a relationship between virtue and learning – the more a woman had of one the less she had of the other. Governesses were only employed for the children of royalty and, in the early 1700's, Young Ladies' Academies were not in being. For the Catholics there were convents and for a very few French girls there was Madame de Maintenon's unique and pioneering establishment at St. Cyr which had the astonishing distinction of having a play written for it by Racine to be performed by the pupils.

c. 1710   1715   1705   c. 1710

Children's Dress

PLATE IX

Fashionable Dress

1731–1735

With the death of Louis XIV there died also a whole astounding epoch of pomp and grandeur. Like his extreme character, art, architecture and manners had taken on a heavy gloss that cracked and faded as it outlived its span. When the old king died Europe breathed again, threw off its autumn colours of gold, reds and browns and stepped straight into spring.

Great as the contrast appears to be, the culture of the gay and graceful 18th century was, nevertheless, built upon the sombre foundations of the 17th.

Humanitarianism had begun to penetrate the consciousness of the individual after the horrors of war in the mid-17th century, perhaps from the example of the small minority practising the religious principles of humility and charity. It began to dawn on man that others might share his emotions of pride and fear and resent being tortured, fleeced and superseded. Brutality and licentiousness and the attitude of every-man-for-himself could only be bridled by a self-discipline which, it was concluded, could be achieved by training and adherence to a certain code of manners. This code we have learnt to accept as etiquette, and the 17th century brought it to a fine art. The practice of greeting by bowing and shaking the right hand made one a little less wary in those sword-happy days, and the new little courtesies to down-trodden women saved a lot of nagging and unpleasantness. The idea, though elementary, made life a little less messy and rough and, adroitly put over by privileged society, succeeded in erecting another barrier between the social classes. The snag arose when the ritual outweighed the purpose and a rule governed every action, the question of precedence being particularly tricky. The showy clothes, feathered hats and sweeping dresses were very much the outcome of this surface polish of manners. Nevertheless, the airs were there and it only needed the 18th century to add the graces.

Much the same could be said for the arts. The Rococo style which followed the bloated Baroque used the same principles of design – curves instead of classical straight lines, superimposed decoration with no relation to the object – but diminished the scale, lightened the colour and developed charm where the latter had projected weight and grandeur.

Although the art expresses to perfection the butterfly spirit of the French 18th century with no high-falutin ideas as to its value to posterity ('*Après nous le déluge*', said Madame de Pompadour, its most enthusiastic exponent) and its decoration is inclined to peel and the mirrors to blister, it did embrace every aspect of daily life and produced a standard of craftsmanship in furniture, porcelain and textiles that has hardly ever been excelled.

It did not take the other nations long to throw off their weight of pomp and join in the fun with France, and by the 1720's dainty palaces and pavilions were sprouting in all the capitals of Europe. Every object was framed in the famous broken curves, scrolls and shells while flying cupids were much in evidence – looking much less respectable than their ancestors, the Baroque 'putti'. With a sure touch the originators of the Rococo matched the delicate decoration with a new set of colours inspired by a spring bouquet – clear pinks and yellows, celestial blues and the tender greens of fresh shoots. Never was there such a get-together between designers and craftsmen to produce a perfect entity, or so unique an occasion in the history of costume, when the styles appear due less to the whim of an outstanding personality than to the deliberate intention of artist-designers. France, who, it must be said, was the first to adopt and develop the Rococo, was prompt to design and produce the subtle and pretty materials the new fashions demanded.

By 1720 woman had relaxed from the stiff and angular shape of the previous fashion. There is nothing that woman likes better than to lounge about in a sloppy garment and only dress up for occasions, hence the shifts, sacks, teagowns and tents that crop up so often in the history of woman's dress. So it is not surprising that the style that caught on in a big way, as soon as the public attitude to deportment relaxed, was the *sacque*, a new version of that useful little number, the house dress of the late 17th century. It had been revived by a Parisian actress in 1703 as a discreet method of conveying the condition of the heroine she was playing, and was found so entrancing that it was exploited anew, as a perfect garment for women in the new freer and easier society. The *sacque*, as the name implies, was an enveloping overdress cut all in one piece, with a cunning arrangement of pleats and seams to give fullness in the skirt but to fit the top of the figure. The back widths were pleated flat into a band at the neck and allowed to flow free to the hem in a train, while the material at either side was flattened to the ribs, seamed, and sewn to a lining to give the appearance of a fitted bodice. From the waist the material flowed out again over full or hooped petticoats. The front was flat-pleated from the shoulders, in the same way as the back, but was darted under the bust and caught to the under-bodice at the waist. This overdress was worn over a fancy corset and a petticoat of the same material. The line of the back pleats made tight corsetting less essential and the graceful effect can be judged from Watteau's lovely versions that gave it the name by which it is known today. What it looked like, less ideally, was summed up by the coarse English in the term 'the trollop', or 'slammerkin'. A small head now made the perfect apex to the new triangular shape of the figure with only tiny caps or posies to enhance the closely dressed natural curls.

Man, too, emerged from his obliterating head-covering and board-like clothes. With spreading coat skirts, his head followed the same principle as that of the woman. Wigs were still essential to a well turned-out appearance as they could be duplicated, dressed on a stand and ready to put on as the finishing touch to the toilet. They were dressed close to the head with the back hair pushed into a bag or allowed to hang in one or more curls tied back with a flat bow. The rather bare look of the collarless coat and plain band of the neck-cloth was relieved by the ends of the ribbon-bow being carried round the neck and fastened to one side by a jewel. Coats, now plainer, relied on cut for elegance, fitting sharply to the waist then springing out in several pleats at the side seams, being reinforced with horsehair or buckram linings. With a slit up the back, sitting was more graceful and less difficult than it looks from a standing figure.

The social arts were most important in this picturesque period, dancing, in particular, being extremely popular. The visiting dancing master was invaluable in keeping one up to the mark, not only in the latest step but in the niceties of social etiquette, as he mixed with the rich and influential and was as well up as the Edwardian English butler in the intricacies of upper-class behaviour. Man was no less eager to escape from the burden of formal clothes than woman and, in England, certainly in the late 17th century, had spent as much time as possible in a dressing- or house-gown that was probably first worn on some colonial verandah by an English nabob. The 18th century version was shorter, more fitted and no longer of the printed Indian cotton in which it first made its appearance. Altogether it had less of the bedroom air about it. The idea of winding a scarf into a neat turban round the head most likely came from the same oriental source. As wigs, for continuous wear, were hot, and shaven skulls were cold as well as unsightly, the fashion was welcomed by young and old alike and completed to perfection the picture of elegant ease.

1735   1731   1735

Fashionable Dress

PLATE X

Domestic Dress

1730–1738

Life was not all lounging, dancing and gallantry as might be suspected from the Watteaus and Lancrets of the early 18th century. The high life that made such charming subjects for those pictures was confined to the courts and aristocracy of Europe, and the less exotic milieu had another, though equally pleasant, appearance which we may see in the more modest interiors of Chardin's paintings. In France, for instance, where the social strata were rigidly defined, the rich middle class was not admitted to the rarified atmosphere of the nobility who resented any impinging on their inherited position. The *bourgeoisie*, with no choice, took refuge with their hurt pride in an attitude of moral righteousness and made their own way of life in a comfortable but simpler manner.

There was a much smaller gay and high life in hybrid Britain where a preponderance of families, even in the upper class, had risen by means of marriage, politics or money and whose attitude, through religion or self-satisfaction, held a certain primness towards extravagance and glamour. The British sourness and instant criticism of French fashion has a long history, from the rude little marginal illumination on the subject of French head-dresses in a copy of Froissart's manuscript of the 15th century, to the acid caricatures of Hogarth and Gilray in the 18th. It is possible that with the exception of a few cosmopolitan individuals the majority of the English people looked very much like the sober middle-class French or Dutch. Credit must be given to them in that they were the first to choose clothes suitable to the conditions of their way of life.

The British court, from the time of William III, had certainly given no example or encouragement to its subjects to shine sartorially. So secluded did these monarchs become that the average citizen had to rely on the word of his parliament that he still had a sovereign on the throne.

Locally made material was a strong factor governing the appearance of the English people. Small towns and villages were still self-supporting in the reign of George I and supplied the crafts and textiles needed for all but the most luxurious mansion or extravagant town dweller. No factories cluttered the agricultural land and the spinning of yarn was done by the women and children in the cottages. With no interference from nosey School Board inspectors they were kept so busy that Daniel Defoe remarked that it was a matter of great satisfaction that even a child of five could keep itself. Most cottages had their looms, in this domestic industry, where the men wove the cloth that was bought by the middleman to be marketed locally or sent to join the huge cargoes of woven cloth exported overseas. Mulberry trees had rather optimistically been distributed over the land to help the silk weavers, many thousands of whom had settled in East Anglia or at Spitalfields in London and whose glinting brocades and taffetas shine in Hogarth's pictures. The industry proceeded profitably and peacefully until the over-enthusiastic and greedy merchants succeeded in tying up the export and import trade into the sort of knots that make such tedious news today. France, too, managed to throttle her industry, but in a more intricate way. Her home-produced textiles were of the first and most sumptuous quality designed for her own sparkling high life and that of the aspiring courts of other European nations. There was less of the utilitarian product for the peasant and worker, so that when the cheap printed cottons arrived from the East Indian colonies and flooded the market they were snapped up by the over-taxed poorer class and were found so enchanting by the fashionable that a new vogue for simplicity was started and soon brought the local looms to a standstill. Customs laws were hastily enforced, and fines comprising money and the confiscation of the garment (often off the wearer) added to the excitement and confusion.

It is in the more conservative clothes of the French middle class and less adventurous British that we can see the evolution of style more clearly than in the high fashion that seemed to change so abruptly. Women's dresses, in the new vogue for softness and simplicity, had gone back to the sensible shape worn by peasants over the centuries, with the tight, straight bodice, cuffed elbow sleeves and full gathered skirt that replaced the more complicated cut of the funnel-shaped, gored skirt of the time of Louis XIV. They were, more practically, shorter, and unless the wearer was of a flighty turn of mind were worn over petticoats and not stiff hoops. Soft muslin fichus draped the neck and were drawn down to hide the front closure of the bodice.

In a fashion that died hard the dress was sometimes drawn up to the waist and fastened in four places, either for decorative purposes or as a protection to the material against muddy roads. The striped fabric often used for the underskirts shows the homespun nature of the material – stripes being the easiest form of variation in hand-weaving.

Even the old Dutch négligé jacket had a renewed life, lasting well into the century, in the form of a short overdress that was often made of the forbidden Indian printed cotton. The shorter skirts revealed the new delightful shoes that the high fashion had introduced. With slightly lifting pointed toes, sometimes backless like modern mules, and high, shaped heels and ribbon bows or rosettes, they are as much a symbol of the 18th century as the square-toed high-fronted fashion was of the 17th. Their originators must have been equally pleased with the model, as copies were made in Sèvres or Meissen china as ornaments.

Another useful garment, refurbished, was the demure palatine, or bust concealer, introduced by the prudish Duchess of Orleans many years earlier. The new version was a dainty little cape that reached just to the elbow and was sometimes slightly longer at the back. This, in muslin or lace, was very popular as a house garment but in cloth or taffeta made a graceful fashion for outdoor wear.

The domestic woman, especially the English housewife, never felt dressed without a cap: only the great court beauties flaunted uncovered hair. The new tiny caps were sometimes tied under the chin with the narrow frills (that dipped slightly over the forehead) prolonged, as lappets, over each ear. For outdoor wear a lower version of the old high hood covered the white cap, or, most becoming of all, the country-woman's shallow, wide-brimmed hat was adopted for general wear.

Altogether, the fashions of this period show a greater feeling towards comfort (which we gather from the shorter skirts and the small girl's cosy muff) and harmonious proportion, with less exaggeration than costume had shown for many a day or was to show a few decades hence.

1732　　　　　　　　　　1730　　　　　1730　　　　　　　　　　1738

Domestic Dress

PLATE XI

Fashionable Day Dress

The next picture is an excellent example not only of the evolution of the pannier dress but of the obstinate British habit of adopting a foreign custom and adapting it so vigorously that all alien elements are safely eliminated. A modern variation on this theme with a fortuitous twist for the adapters is in the matter of mini skirts which, contrary to belief, did not originate in this country but due to the energetic efforts of a new extrovert population were not only accepted but so acclimatized that they have been acknowledged as the brain-child of British designers and exploited as such to enormous profit. There was no commercial intention in the 18th century. It was merely the wish to be in the latest fashion while making it suitable for a rather different way of life from that of its originators. Time and again the French have borrowed ideas from the English and produced something so much more provocative than the original that the final product has had to be toned down when it made its way back across the English Channel. Relations have become rather strained at times even for those pining to wear the latest that Paris could provide. In the latter part of the 17th century a coterie of smart Parisiennes, concerned for the appearance of their out-of-touch English sisters, had started sending regularly to London models of the latest fashions on intricately dressed dolls. So popular were these mannequins that over a long period of years not even a war prevented them crossing the Channel. Kind though the initial thought might have been, it was also an excellent boost for French trade and it was unfortunate that some distrustful English characters should have begun to suspect that French humour had got the better of tact and that 'Pandora' was not always in the latest fashion. The little jest of Paris designers in the Second World War, producing fashions, it has been confessed, to make the heavy German client look ridiculous, prompts one to think there was much in the suspicions.

In the interchange of ideas pannier dresses, too, made their way backwards and forwards between the two countries. Wide stiffened petticoats undoubtedly started their career in the theatre, society lacking any personality or originality at this period. The French company who made them such a universal success generously admitted that they had picked up the idea while playing in London. The current fashion being so tame it is quite possible that the ladies of the very popular English theatre had livened up their shape in this outstanding manner.

Whoever had the first idea, it was taken up with rapture by the fashionable and with fury by the moralists, who preached sermons against it, wrote pamphlets and even legislated against it. With wearisome regularity anything new and eccentric is proclaimed immoral but, after it has become accepted, discarding it becomes downright wanton. Panniers started a long fashionable life as 'guilt disguisers', but many years later when Marie Antoinette was heartily sick of them she was accused of every kind of impropriety for leaving them off.

Hooped petticoats were no new invention : it was the peculiar shape they eventually became that aroused such ire. Very early in the century iron or wooden rings had been threaded through slots in a funnel-shaped petticoat to hold out the heavy material then used for skirts, and were quite a rational and invisible part of the dress. At their re-introduction in the 1720's they were anything but invisible : they altered the entire shape of the wearer.

The sane but rather timid fashion after 1710 had at first been gingered up by a round hooped petticoat, but as this looked too like the previous old fashion, without its character, the next obvious variation was to change the circle to an oval by tying in the more flexible cane hoops from back to front. A woman then walked in a cage, not only ringed round, but criss-crossed by tapes and flattened back and front. The whole structure could be made of wood or cane taped horizontally and vertically together but a more comfortable and less erratic garment was produced when whalebone took the place of the heavier stiffeners and was threaded through tucks in a linen petticoat. There was such a demand for the new material that the Dutch set up a whaling station solely to provide for this purpose and made a small fortune over the years.

The early shape, through being the same length all round, had the intriguing habit of tilting up at the sides and could be flaunted to show the ankles and pretty red-heeled shoes, but even that advantage was jettisoned in the search for further extravagance.

The box shape of the new skirt was so novel that it positively demanded carrying to extremes. The petticoats were then extended and squared off with pads to lift the sides horizontally in two shelves, either as elbow rests or making it imperative to hold the arms stiffly forward in front of the panniers. The Frenchwoman covered herself and the whole contraption in the *sacque* dress that was, indeed, called the '*robe à la française*', and yet managed to reveal a feminine shape by the nature of her corsetting which allowed a soft rounded bosom to swell over the curved front busks. The Englishwoman counteracted any such tendency by firmly lacing her corset up the back and presenting a long flat front to the world. The trim English bodice, itself, often had a back closure and was held down by being attached firmly to the skirts. The long lean look of the bodice was intensified by a white kerchief being pulled down narrowly and held in place by one strap or more across the front, which later developed into criss-cross lacing. Tiers of graduated bows were much more to French taste.

Aprons and caps were always dear to the more homely Englishwoman who clung to them no matter what the occasion. This conservative domestic habit was particularly infuriating to Beau Nash, trying to give tone and sophistication to society in Bath: taking a strong line with the Duchess of Queensberry he tore off her costly apron and flung it to the ground in front of the entire company at an assembly. Very seldom was an Englishwoman seen with an uncovered head. Small mob caps gathered at the nape of the neck, or triangles of lace and lawn, topped closely dressed hair, but the favourite style was the cap with frills that dipped slightly over the forehead and continued in lappets left loose on the shoulders or tied under the chin. These were particularly fetching when covered by the flat hats in fine straw or silk in the deliberately simple shepherdess style that had become the vogue through the excursions into Arcadia by the fashionable painters.

The slightly bedroom look of the French *sacque* did not endear itself very quickly to our straight-laced countrywoman but the wide panniers that accentuated the clear outline and emphasized their withdrawn attitude were an instant and increasing success. The difficulty of allowing enough material to cover the enormous width of the panniers in ample folds was catered for by the pleats, back and front, from the shoulders of the *sacque* dress, and even then sometimes had to open down the front over an under-skirt. The trim bodice-and-skirt line presented a problem that was neatly overcome by continuing the fullness at the waist laterally, into the side seams running along the top of the panniers. English skirts were inclined to be less fussy than the French fashions but when worn with a front opening the under-skirt was often of very fine quilting.

The difficulties of precedence can be imagined when every woman was encased in a square cage. On State occasions double the space was necessary to prevent the Queen from being obscured by those of less degree – and so on, down the scale of personages of importance.

In spite of embarrassments the shape kept its popularity until well after the mid-18th century and became, on account of the grand style it gave to the wearer, official court dress in all the capitals of Europe, only being abolished in Britain as late as the 1830's.

1744   c. 1744   c. 1752

Fashionable Day Dress

PLATE XII

English Children's Dress

1740–1744

The English do not appear to have become aware of children as individuals until the 1740's. Previously children had been treated as less capable grown-ups, a nuisance and an encumbrance, and parents had little pleasure from the patter of small feet or the nonsense of childish behaviour. The main idea in child upbringing was to ignore the tiresome, dependent period by dressing him like an adult, imparting knowledge as quickly as possible and breaking his wilful spirit. Judging by the only English pictures we have to go by or letters from conscientious parents, they succeeded remarkably well. Let us hope that it was for want of good painters that the English child looks so deprived. The liberal Dutch had earlier shown a sensitivity towards youth, as we gather from their 17th century genre pictures which were followed by the French in charming interiors by Chardin and Boucher.

The new attitude to children may have come about because we were losing them so fast in the early 18th century. In the upper classes the habit, through laziness and custom, of feeding babies artificially (at a time of total ignorance of hygiene), and in the working classes the effects of gin, starvation and disease, made infant mortality distressingly high. Consequently the little survivors of the rich were guarded and spoilt more than was good for them and those of the poor were abandoned on the streets until conscience began to stir, in London at least, and the good Captain Coram gave them shelter in his Foundling Hospital. The solid middle class had already realized the dangers of town life to their families and had moved them away from the open sewers and smoke to the more salubrious air of the villages around London. Country children had a greater expectation of life, and as the custom developed of putting babies of the better-off families to nurse with strong respectable village women their chances of survival improved, but it is hardly surprising that filial affection suffered in consequence. Royal children experienced an even more extraordinary upbringing by being wrenched from their families at an early age and set up in separate establishments presided over by governesses, nurses and tutors. The waste of money and natural affection seems to have escaped these otherwise intelligent people.

It is with the advent of the humanist Hogarth and the gentle narrative painter Highmore that we begin to see a little more cheer in the life of the English child. Brutal though the goings-on were on the streets of London the children appear to have joined in the fun and even the high-class child, though still sedate, has games and toys in plenty.

It is too much to expect that attitudes would have changed in every aspect, suitable dress for children being a peculiarly blind spot until such a short time ago. The poor child, unless at the expense of the Charity Schools, wore cut-down grown-up clothes and the well-to-do child miniature replicas of fashionable adult dress.

Babies were trussed up like cocoons in the earnest belief that bindings straightened limbs, and if they refused to die from germs they often did so, later, from lack of air or from restriction. Small boys, up to the age of four or so, were indistinguishable from their sisters in long skirts with sashes, only being put into breeches as they left off nappies. It was not until 1760 that a very small boy appears in the long loose trousers which, ironically, became acknowledged as the most comfortable wear for men in the 19th century.

It is the toys that tell us so much about the life of children at this period. Rocking-horses had been made much earlier but of solid wood and safely low on the ground. The new models were much more excitingly like the real animal and adventurously high. Tin soldiers made their first appearance as is natural in an age of national military pride, and we see the games of cards and hazard that were proving so enthralling in the grown-up world. For out-of-doors, little go-carts to be pulled by older brothers and sisters were much in vogue, and windmills in paper amused the babies much as they do, in plastic, to-day. But it is the dolls that tell us so much of what we want to know of the dress of the time. The little garments were so faithfully made and with such skill that it is possible to see not only what a small girl wore but how, of course, her mother's clothes were made. Underclothes consisted of chemises and petticoats; the latter, for warmth, were quite narrow and hung close to the figure under the wide panniers. The panniers themselves were not merely a straight piece of gathered material held out by wire but were cut in the correct wide shape and stiffened by graduated hoops of whalebone. Small pads were placed on top of the sides to lift the skirts into the fashionable square shape, and innumerable tapes pulled in the hoops. Girls' dresses were made to look as nearly like a woman's as possible and stays were worn very early to reduce the ribs and the unruly bulge at the waist. Skirts were full and gathered with a jaunty lift at the sides where the panniers tilted up. Bodices, fitted with stiffened seams, were usually fastened down the back but the effect of a stomacher was achieved by making the front section of the bodice of a contrasting material and allowing the stiffened point to lie over the apron and skirt.

The strong patriarchal influence of the Dissenters may have been responsible for the continued covering of women's heads and it is a wonder that English women were ever famed for their hair. Even small girls wore the ubiquitous cap – tiny affairs in muslin or lace with a little frivolity in a wreath of flowers or for grand occasions even a feather.

The eldest son was, of course, the pampered darling of the family. With freedom at home, the power to rise above savage bullying at a Public School or the polish added by accomplishments taught at the private academies for the sons of gentlemen, an English boy very early developed that independence and arrogance that has been such a sore spot of envy and irritation to other nations ever since.

By 1740 men's coats were becoming much closer-fitting with a trace of the cutaway look that developed a decade later. Unbuttoned and with less stiffening the fronts fell away naturally at the sides. Decoration was reduced to military braiding and variations on the shape of the wide cuffs. Waistcoats were shorter and fastened at the waist and plain neck-cloths for everyday wear were tucked into the open top and showed above the still collarless coat.

While the older man was now to be seen more often in a suit made all from the same material, the younger bloods favoured lighter and brighter colours for their breeches. Three-cornered hats had a long life and, according to fashionable information of the period, were a good indication of a man's character. The front point too high in the air gave away the wearer as a rustic 'gawky'; tassels and buttons, too great an affectation; while hats edged round with gold binding belonged to the brothers of the turf !

1742   c. 1740   c. 1744   1742   1742

English Children's Dress

PLATE XIII

Court Dress

1751–1759

It is doubtful if any woman has ever left such an indelible mark on history as la Pompadour. They have become legends by causing wars, stirred emotions or encouraged thought by beauty or talent, but none has combined all these activities with such taste and visual sensibility that her name has become the symbol not only for the life of a period but the look. An iron will and stamina are other qualities to which Madame de Pompadour could lay claim, since at that period, unfortunately, to have real influence on events it was necessary to become the mistress of the King of France. Modern film stars and pop singers are luckier in having more scope with no strings. Ethically debased though the purpose was, we must be grateful that the political faction, who saw her potentialities and had her trained from early youth in all the social accomplishments as a fifth column at court, developed talents in her that she was able to put to wider use than the amusement of a clot of a king.

Jeanne de Pompadour did not make her environment at Versailles : the exclusive, hot-house atmosphere was there as a legacy from the days of Louis XIV, but from the time she entered court circles her exquisite and refining influence prevented it from descending to blatant vulgarity. The very peculiar nature of the French court, exclusive and extravagant with a wealth of original talent to supply its needs, made it possible to produce a pattern of life enviable to the rest of the materialistic world. The only drawback for that birth-conscious nation was that fate had denied it the right type of personalities as heirs to the throne. It is ironic that the woman who enabled it to keep its comfortable lead was a member of the hated middle class and a thorn in the side of every aristocrat forced to acknowledge her position. Having been divorced so long from things spiritual, the French court was blissfully unaware of matters of the soul and could happily devote its entire energies to the enjoyment of physical pleasures, and Madame de Pompadour was just the girl to cultivate this pursuit to a fine art. The perfection of the Rococo period is purely

material. Its painters, by a curious coincidence, were the offspring of skilled craftsmen, and although the sublime is lamentably absent from their work they have left us a perfect record of physical joy and the little details of the surroundings that make it appear so entrancing.

With the accent on sensual pleasure no stone was left unturned to enhance physical beauty. Small and delicate herself, Madame de Pompadour saw to it that by direct encouragement of artists and craftsmen a suitable frame was made for her personality, which was so compelling that even the most antipathetic of the French nobles were soon following her taste in Sevres porcelain, her dainty furniture and, above all, her choice of material and dress. This veered towards simplicity in a very decorated period, and her famous hairstyle must have put a strain on all but those with the suitable features.

The old *sacque* dress that had done such good service over the past two decades was still in favour as a négligé but was too droopy and obscuring to display the spruce figures that now made themselves noticed in the fashionable world. The attractive sweep of the Watteau pleats was so dearly beloved that it lasted till the 1780's but the well-boned bodice was now made to fit closely, all round the body, with a lining under the pleats, and was cut separately from the front widths of the skirt which was gathered tightly into the waist. The overdress effect remained the favourite style but no longer hung loose like a coat, the fronts being fastened to the stomacher, or underbodice, which lay over the under-skirt in a sharp point and was, in France, generally decorated with rows of graduated bows. Corsets were universally worn, whaleboned and beautifully fitted in small sections to assist the smooth look of the long lean torso. Sleeves were a triumph of design. These had been long-fitting ones trimmed with lace frills at the wrist, elbow sleeves with rows of lace ruffles from just below the shoulder-line, or, most usual, long bell sleeves turned back to make a cuff, or folded upon themselves, more narrowly in front, to give the appearance of a pleated, shaped cuff over the lawn and lace of the chemise. The most beautiful line, which perfected the silhouette of the whole figure – the narrow top swelling out and swept back – was the fitting elbow sleeve with one or more circularly cut, gathered frill, narrow in width in front and falling longer at the back to be repeated with lace frills of the same cut underneath. The favourite trimming was ruching of various widths, which finished every edge and ornamented the skirts in interwoven designs.

The encumbrance and inconvenience of the great square panniers gave way in the 1750's to a softer more manageable line, by means of a hooped knee-length petticoat which was quickly followed by the bright idea of boned side-pads tied round the waist like a bustle over each hip. The wide panniers were then only retained for full ceremonial court wear when, it appears, intense physical discomfort for the sake of prestige was meekly endured by all. Black pages dressed in the latest European fashion and treated like pet monkeys were considered a quaint and amusing foil for fragile white beauty. The thriving French slave trade – though not in the rosy position of the English with the shipment of half the world's demands for this rich commodity – made the supply abundant and cheap.

Male clothes underwent a considerable change half way through the 18th century. Gone were the ballet-dance lines of the Watteau period and, although still decorated, coats began to take on the business-like and close-fitting cut of modern clothes. The wide stiffened skirts of the coat had proved themselves a nuisance to all but exquisites. The man of action, especially in England where riding was of such importance, had already begun to turn the corners and button them out of the way. This revealed a contrasting lining of which much play was made in army uniforms and later led to the idea of turning back the neck as lapels. The cut-off effect was found so convenient that very shortly all coats were cut away, the fullness at the side seams reduced to a single pleat and the whole garment given a swept-back line. Following the slimmer cut of the body, sleeves became narrower, cuffs and pockets smaller and the decoration reduced to braid, frogs and tassels. The waistcoat which was still embroidered or of rich brocade was becoming shorter as the century advanced. Altogether a man began to look more alert and less like a lounger, but it was some time before the more decorative French put themselves into plain suits of good English cloth. That it was not all eternal summer in this halcyon period is given away by a few pictures in which full fur linings appear as edging to the smart cutaway coats.

One facet of the diamond-cut character of Madame de Pompadour that is not so well known is the intelligent curiosity that led her to encourage the writers of Diderot's famous French encyclopaedia. As a woman of the people she was excited by their inflammatory, radical contributions (little knowing that they would inspire the spirit of the Revolution that swept away the social order of which she had been such an ornament) but she was more immediately concerned with the information imparted by their articles on general knowledge. They not only widened the education of her own generation but have left us a complete picture of the science, industry and domestic life of the 18th century, and as far as costume is concerned there can be no argument as to how wigs were dressed or coats were cut in the time of Louis XV.

c. 1751   1758   1759   c. 1752

Mrs. Loveit

Court Dress

PLATE XIV

Fashionable Dress

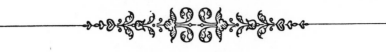

1760–1768

With the rise of a host of good painters the English scene opens up before us, still a little high-class (owing to the sort of prices demanded by Gainsborough, Reynolds, Ramsay and others) but domestic as well as aristocratic and showing people as they really must have looked enjoying the everyday pursuits of town and country life. Hogarth lived till 1764 to describe so intimately the doings of the lesser folk. At the same time French painters lost interest in the domestic scene and, except in highly idealized fashion engravings of rich home life, concentrated on vast canvasses of grand occasions. This is a very clear indication of the diverse life led by the two nations : French aristocracy on the one hand, sporting in rarified seclusion, and the English on the other, spending more time in the country or getting together in the county towns as well as in London for their amusements at which, although the gentry had privilege of first place, the company was most democratically mixed. This delightful situation was only killed at the rise of the rich non-conformist middle class in the 19th century, partly through their kill-joy attitude to pleasure and partly due to the new snobbery that made the upper classes withdraw through fear of an invasion of their privileges. It has taken another hundred years for the situation to even out somewhat, by which time taste has changed and the population grown too vast for comfortable mass amusement. Public entertainment was all the thing in the 18th century. Spas rose as an excuse for a holiday to repair the ravages of high living and as social meeting places for isolated country gentry. London life was very gay, catering for all tastes and incomes, with cards and gaming as exciting and dangerous pursuits, the theatre industry booming and lovely pleasure gardens for alfresco amusement. Ranelagh and the Spring Gardens at Vauxhall were opened in the late 17th century and despite a few lapses into disreputability they remained popular pleasure spots all through the 18th century, providing concerts, dancing and fireworks in a delightful setting of tree-lined walks and fountains, with fairy-lit shrubberies for amorous dallying. Drenched garden fêtes, arranged for a single occasion in later years, are the sad outcome of that typically British characteristic of optimistic nostalgia that pines to enjoy the beauty of its gardens and vainly hopes for a return of the serene climate of the 18th century.

All this alfresco gambolling was part of the rustic craze (in which clothes played a large part) that became so popular in both England and France but from rather different reasons.

In England it arose from a genuine love of the country life and, as already mentioned, the mixing of all sorts and conditions in places of amusement. The studied innocence and milk-maid dresses of the lively ladies of the town, on pleasure and business bent at Vauxhall, suited the atmosphere to perfection and were often taken as a model by their no less lively but more distinguished fellow revellers from Mayfair. Then, there were all the lovely light materials, dainty printed cottons and muslin from India, and now being made in our own Lancashire, that cried out to be made into the country-girl styles. The craze went deep in England and lasted alongside the high fashion to the end of the century.

The wide panniers went out of favour by the 1750's and left a softer line with a little fullness only over the hips. The figure on the left of Plate XIV illustrates how successfully and attractively the peasant style was adapted for everyday wear. The tightly drawn-down kerchief emphasizing the slim English bodice, together with the long straight apron, were of the most delicate embroidered muslin, and the shallow hat was of the finest straw, but the effect of the whole ensemble was the same as that of the milk-maid or strawberry seller.

It was an escape, on the other hand, for the social elite of France from the stifling monotony of Court regime that brought about the rustic trend. French painters had made the Arcadian simple life very tempting to the bored sophisticates of Paris and Versailles, but the Trianons and shepherdesses sporting in the chequered shade that resulted from it look a trifle self-conscious and theatrical.

By a strange paradox, at the same time as the Englishwoman had established a mode both attractive and suitable to her activities she suddenly caught up with the French high fashion and for all formal occasions went all-out to show what a decoration she could be to it. The lavish use of lace and the shape of the sleeves, even on the simple dress, are an indication that the Pandora mannequin from Paris was now in favour. The *sacque* dress had a further 'new look' with a raised waist-line, and without the bulky panniers to hold it out it showed the swept-back trend that is discernible in both men's and women's clothes. Spiral ruching and frilled underskirts all went to make dresses more complicated in the gradual tendency away from the clean line of the early Rococo period. Hairstyles, too, began to fall in line with French fashion. As they became less severe and rose higher the Englishwoman actually abandoned her eternal cap and coiled her locks high on her head with flowers or a swathed turban on top. An accessory that was curiously prevalent and enduring in both countries was the tiny neck frill which quite usurped the place of a necklace over a period of some forty years. It could be fastened by a bow, *à la* Pompadour, or with an exquisite brooch, and the only alternative even for the richest woman appears to have been a small choker or a bare neck.

Men's coats began to develop collars and lapels in the 1760's, first by the top being cut higher and closer to the neck and gradually turned over. In the same way waistcoats, which were becoming shorter and shorter, started to be double-breasted with the extra width turned back as lapels. Except for grand occasions, when beautiful brocades and embroidered silks and velvets were still worn, coats were plain and only trimmed with braid and buttons, the latter of great variety and beauty. Cuffs became smaller as the decade advanced and gradually disappeared altogether, their place being taken by the modern buttoned slit. The older figure in Plate XIV would be a man of some substance, judging by the *London Chronicle* which stated that 'the beaux of St James' wear their hats under their arms while the beaux of Moorfield's Mall (a less exclusive region) cock theirs over the right or left eye'.

It was about 1765 that wigs were noticeably less worn by the ordinary man. The natural hair was then treated like a wig and dressed higher with powder for full dress wear. It was the lull before the storm as a few years later the Macaronis, protesting against the dullness of man's appearance, proved to what fantastic heights hairdressing could reach.

c. 1760   c. 1768   c. 1760   c. 1760

Lady Woodvill   *Parson*   *Lady Townley*

Fashionable Dress

PLATE XV

Sporting Dress

1760–1778

Britain may have produced Shakespeare, ruled the waves and carried on wars most successfully all over the globe, but the thing that really mattered and held it together through the ages was sport. The playing fields of Eton are said to have won us Waterloo but without the hunting and the shooting and the village cricket greens that preceded them there might not have been the flower of British aristocracy to perform so creditably in 1815. For sport in Britain had been the great mixer and the common ground on which all could share the fun. Bottle-throwing on football fields, horse-doping and screaming fits in the boxing ring are the nasty results of greed and mass non-participation. Like the Constitution we have so proudly offered to other nations, sport goes back a long way in our evolution. Early English manuscripts illustrate a pre-occupation with quite recognizable games, and the hunting and hawking Barons had their foot-sloggers to be in at the kill, but general participation in field sports came when the fox took the place of the deer as prey (through deforestation and land enclosure) and every Tom, Dick and Harry with a grey mare could follow the chase. If pop songs are anything to go by, the 'hunting horn' and 'the fox in the morning', hammered out with pewter pots in ale-house or Manorial hall, were the engrossing theme of the 18th century as 'heart' and 'blues' are of the mid-20th.

The muzzle-loading gun had added zest and danger to the enthralling occupation of killing birds, an activity indulged in by other nations but a positive passion with the British. Systematic slaughter was the order of the day for the grand house parties assembled in the great Manors for a season and a surfeit of field sports, but the solitary man, land-owner, farmer or poacher could be seen keeping his hand in at any time, all over England's pleasant land; with the unpredictable weapon at his disposal he needed to, as it could never be relied upon to explode at the right moment – which in itself was a matter for tricky calculation owing to the gun's slow action. The dogs, too, had an added ritual to their training,

dropping to the ground at the order 'down charge' during the hazardous process of reloading. On the whole they all managed pretty well, with crack shots averaging a bag of eighty per cent of the shots so laboriously fired.

As this was the time of the easy mixing of all classes so it was of sections of society. The political, literary and fashionable coterie were one and the same set, enjoying the same pursuits, and a Charles James Fox or a Richard Sheridan were equally at home in the House, at Drury Lane or on the hunting field.

Sport more than anything else dictated the Englishman's costume. Whereas the continental chase brought out something much more fancy, with extra trimming, heavier boots and a more dramatic curl to the hat (a turn-out that has been a godsend to pantomime transformation scenes and the classical ballet), the hunt and the shoot in Britain produced something much more practical. Having become used to the comfortable and hard-wearing cloth coat and preferring the sporting life to all others, he took it with him in a glorified fashion to the clubs and boudoirs of Mayfair. Breeches became longer due to this influence, to tuck into top boots that were more frequently worn for sport, though gaiters and thick over-stockings were comfortable enough for shooting. Coats remained very much the same for ten years or more. The large cuffs gradually disappeared, the waistcoat lifted still higher and the neck rose to be turned over into a collar that became the high fashion and can be seen on the golfer of the last years of the 1780's. This Scottish gentleman is also wearing the tight, single-breasted fashion that took the place of the more practical double-breasted sports coat of an earlier decade. From it developed the short, tight garment of the last years of the century, which was the nearest that could be managed to the Greek and Stuart tunics that the rather muddled romantic-cum-classical ideal made all the rage. The extra front widths of the golfer's coat are buttoned decoratively back into full-length lapels giving it a military air, though it was, in fact, a natty idea for a distinctive club uniform. Golf, even if the Anglo-Saxons can be seen playing something suspiciously like it, was not introduced into Scotland until the 15th century and was brought south by those ardent players, the Stuarts. Exiled Scots in the 18th century, lacking their own courses, played on the wide and open Blackheath. The caddie still wears the long, cuffed coat that must have been worn by the common people throughout the century, and his three-cornered hat is completely outdated by the player's wide-brimmed postillion beaver that took its place in the late 1780's.

What really brought the people of Britain together was the practice – quite incomprehensible to other nations – of team games of which cricket was the most peculiar. For a pastime that has become the all-engrossing summer preoccupation of this country and its late colonies, it is odd that the pundits are not of one mind as to its origin. It was probably played by Stone Age men on the Downs and was certainly enjoyed in the Middle Ages. The wooden stool, called a cricket in the north, used as a wicket appears to be too simple an explanation of this enthralling puzzle. It is, however, satisfactorily agreed that it was largely the game of the illiterate common people till the 18th century owing to the system of scoring by notches, but the aristocratic sportsman of higher degree, itching to have a go while watching a village match, widened its social scope and, in 1743, contemporary surprise noted that 'noblemen, gentlemen and clergy were making butchers, cobblers and tinkers their companions' in this extraordinary game. From the village, county was soon playing county and, still keeping its democratic character, the Lord of the Manor could be a member of a team of which his head gardener was the captain. In the excitement of the game the English aristocrat was quite unconscious of his luck. If, as Sir George Trevelyan has pointed out, the French *noblesse* had been able to play cricket with their peasants they might not have lost their heads. The English countryman would have taken a poor view of executing a man who had made a century for his side.

As sport was the eventual leveller of the status of the sexes, it is interesting to note the progress that the woman of the 18th century had made towards independence before she was thrust back into bondage by the prudish sentimentality of the 19th century. 'Miss Wicket', though a contemporary caricature of 1770, was in fact reality, from the account of a former match played at Guildford in 1745 in which 'the girls bowled, batted, ran and catched as well as most men' to the topmost rung of the social ladder when, in 1779, the Countess of Derby's team played other ladies of quality and fashion.

From the spectators' point of view the game must have had other points than those of skill. Miss Wicket's short, fashionable dress showed more than pretty feet in those runs, and the Dresden Shepherdess hat, perched on frame-mounted hair, was easier on the eye than the men's three-cornered or slouch beavers while illustrating, quite forcibly, that woman need not lose her femininity when playing a man's game. In the trend towards a more natural line in the 1770's the panniers have quite disappeared and the cricketing girl is wearing the short loose jacket, the caraco, which was to become the high note of the 1790's. It is said to have originated in a provincial French fashion but it looks suspiciously like the old *matinée*, that standby of comfort-seeking women through many decades, especially those perspiring in the colonial tropics. The curious shape of the cricket bat was not an unkind reflection on the weight of the girl cricketer. Until the latter part of the century the game was rather different from what it is to-day and the ball was thrown, under-hand, low along the ground, often passing between the two stumps. As the object of the game was to hit one of these the batsman was not out and was allowed to poke the curved end of his bat between the stumps to prevent the wicket keeper 'popping' the ball back.

c. 1760   1778   1778   1770

Sporting Dress

PLATE XVI

Court Dress

1777

Having read the statement that wide panniers had gone out of fashion during the 1750's it will be a surprise to see them used with such extravagance in 1777. The reason for their introduction in the first place is the explanation of their long life. Actresses in the early part of the century had found that the wide-sided skirt made them more noticeable and that the possibilities it gave to dramatic entrances and exits were immense. It was an idea to appeal to the exhibitionist leaders of French fashion who used it to telling effect in the wide spaces of state apartments. When the hair began to rise in the 1770's the combination of the two extremes was the most impressive court dress that has ever been worn, in spite of a weariness for the incommodious garment there seems to have been a tacit agreement in the highest circles of Europe that nothing so fitting or stately could be designed for the purpose and that a change would only be an anticlimax. So it was that, while less cumbersome dresses were being worn both in France and in England, the stiff panniers existed side by side with them for Court and ceremonial occasions. These, in France, were becoming more and more extravagant as another figure made her appearance on the stage of fashion, this time of the right quality of birth and beauty to further the promotion of French culture, in the person of the queen, Marie-Antoinette.

After a poor start, in which even her mother had misgivings as to the cleanliness of her daughter's neck and the royal entourage held her in the same contempt as her husband the Dauphin, she blossomed into a figure of the greatest elegance and personality. Although it is said that she preferred simplicity and comfort in dress to a degree of slovenliness (another failing that called forth a sharp note from her martinet of a mother) the *modistes* and hairdressers of Paris were hardly likely to let slip the opportunity of using her as a gilt-edged mannequin, and her reputed extravagances were mainly due to their pressing importunities. For wear clothes she could — not with the feline ease of a Pompadour whose every detail appears to be a personal choice — but as a beautiful model enjoying wearing fashionable clothes. There are some people who deliberately court criticism in the furtherance of a spectacular career — and get away with it — while others start off on the wrong foot and never manage to fall into step. Poor Marie-Antoinette was one of these unfortunates, and although nobody has denied her charm or wit her every action was a battleground for contention. This made her appearance even more challenging and a still greater asset to the fashion community, for although every new mode she wore was metaphorically pulled to pieces, there were many only too eager to be as provokingly fashionable. The power of the French queen's influence, in a clothes-dominated nation, can be gauged by the satirical title of 'Minister of Fashion' given to her *modiste*, Mademoiselle Bertin, who modestly commenced all observations with 'the Queen and I'.

Fashion's greatest folly came at about the time of the accession of Louis XVI, when hairdressing rose to ludicrous proportions. At its zenith it was said that a smart woman's chin came halfway between her feet and the top of her hair. Having started to raise it by natural means of backcombing and loose coiling the inevitable law of fashion compelled it to continue to the ultimate extreme of exaggeration. Marie-Antoinette had in her *coiffeur* as persuasive a personality as her *modiste* and allowed him — some say participating with him — to perpetrate the wildest creations. So indispensable was this gentleman's services to the queen that it has been said that through waiting for him to join the royal party on their flight to Varennes their plans miscarried, the family was brought back to Paris and the queen lost the head he had served so well.

As there were six hundred other hairstylists now established in Paris the competition in original creations was intense. Horsehair pads were first used and, later, frames to raise the hair to the required height and strength to support the 'feature', known in France as the *pouf au sentiment,* that eye-catching finish to the confection. This called for real invention as no items were barred. Sailing ships, moving birds and whole flower gardens (kept alive by water-filled glass tubes inserted in the hair) vied with one another in the great game of outdoing every new inspiration. For court wear the inevitable white feathers nodded over all. If the wearer lacked sufficient hair to carry up and over the required height, wig frames were made to rest on the head with the natural hair swept up and over it in front and fixed into the false curls on the top and sides. The back hair was arranged in coiled plaits or rows of sausage curls with a few loose locks resting on the neck while the side pieces were curled into large rolls, slanting rather to the back of the ears. The whole erection was covered with pomade and dusted with pounds of rice powder and, with care and a little touching up, was expected to last a week. Dainty, long-handled 'scratchers' were made to give the no doubt necessary relief in these days of infrequent washing, but it was not considered the right thing to use them in public – except in the coarse minor German courts.

This extreme of exaggeration in dress is a reflection of the aimless life passed by high society in the 18th century in which the French were not alone in their frivolity. Even that most modest and retiring of ladies, Queen Charlotte of England, can be seen wearing a head-dress to equal in exaggeration that of the queen of France. Historical events may repeat themselves but throughout the history of costume there is one constant factor : the urge which makes people ignore comfort, discretion or ridicule in the name of fashion. Enormous head-dresses appear outrageous to a modern generation who have accepted, in less leisured times, stiletto heels that ruined floors and trapped hurrying feet, or the contradiction of sleeveless *woollen* dresses designed with complete indifference to the predominantly cold climate.

The British aristocracy had never had it so good as in the late 18th century, and with the distinction that a great many lived sober lives there was a large pleasure-seeking set whose behaviour was as frolicsome as the French. Another difference was that the English did not have royal sanction for their behaviour and were more provincial, making towns like Bath, that had originated for medical reasons, into centres of the most extravagant and expensive amusement.

Sedan chairs were found convenient for short journeys by a vastly increased amusement-seeking community. For attending crowded court ceremonies at St James' or in the steep and narrow streets of Bath these litters were less obstructing than cumbersome carriages. There were privately owned, beautifully decorated equipages carried by liveried bearers, or they could be hired with chairmen, as taxis are to-day. It is strange that at a time when clothes became more bulky these small vehicles should have become so popular, but having made the obstacles human ingenuity managed to circumvent the difficulties. When they were first used hairdressing was quite low but as it rose the roofs of sedan chairs were hinged to lift up, enabling the passenger to enter in comfort and sit down. If the *pouf* was still too high the top had to be left open, revealing the feathers bobbing in time to the bearer's walk. The wide panniers had already proved difficult to negotiate through doorways so slit pockets had been made either side, through the skirt, to enable the wearer to catch strings underneath that pulled the flexible, whalebone hoops forward. Even then it was a tight fit and graceful execution needed a lot of practice.

Men's coats became increasingly slim-fitting in the 1770's. The neck rose into a high-standing collar and the embroidery round the edge of the coat became diagonal in design, two fashions that have survived in ceremonial diplomatic dress. Hat crowns and cocked brims were raised in the general trend towards height and the man's costume of Plate XVI shows the introduction of the narrow-striped material that was to become the typical pattern of the last years of the century.

1777   1777   1777

Court Dress

PLATE XVII

Children's and Manservant's Dress

1780–1787

It is only towards the end of the 18th century that English youth can be said to look natural and happy, the most obvious explanation being their more comfortable clothes. This pleasant revolution came about in a variety of ways, chiefly through the doctrine of Jean-Jacques Rousseau which put into words the yearnings of the more thoughtful of his generation for a less material way of life and advocated a return to, and deeper understanding of Nature. Society was so busy with its rat-race that it took many years before it could realize any alternative existence and only then, perhaps, because life at the top had become so intolerably tedious and a stampede away from artificiality offered fresh interest. Rousseau's passionate philosophy of freedom and untrammelled feeling had unfortunate results in promoting a revolution and stimulating a romantic sentiment in those – alas, many – with less lofty perception. But the nature-study line had less violent repercussions and his interest in children as the spring of human nature led him to concern himself with their conditions and education. He was not alone in his study, for the good Pestalozzi in Switzerland came to the hitherto unheard of conclusion that children could learn through play instead of tears and beatings.

The cultured country-loving and naturally child-loving British took kindly to this new attitude – for it was in England that Rousseau had brushed up his ideas on liberty – and a little more thought and understanding was given to the interests and feelings of the young with less emphasis on curbing their natural inclinations. There are so many beautiful paintings, at about this time, of distinguished mothers with radiant children that it is difficult to believe that the happiness was all in the artists' imagination.

In the enthusiasm of a new experiment some parents rather overdid the indulgence. The father of Charles James Fox refused to have his son's spirit broken, adding that 'the world would do that business fast enough', with the result that his brilliant son lacked the self-discipline that would have made him of greater value to his country. The same indulgence to arrogant manners extended to the Public Schools, where it was now the custom for the sons of gentry to pass a few years and where, schoolmaster flogging having become less violent, the freedom of uncurbed animal spirits intensified the bullying of one another.

Boys matured very quickly in an age where they were allowed the activities of an adult life. Participation in military campaigns was thought quite suitable for boys of high degree, and the experience of naval life must have quickly taken the bloom off a beardless cheek. The Grand Tour, accompanied by a tutor, was the acknowledged climax of a young man's education and doubtless offered much in the way of excitement in the dangers of travel if, otherwise, the ancient culture of Europe proved rather a bore. The 'poor' child matured equally fast, as he was a wage-earner before he was ten. Even though he worked in his village home he had the open fields and moors to play on, in the blissful pause before the Industrial Revolution enticed and trapped him in the mills.

There were plenty of playmates as families were large. In the most aristocratic, such as the Devonshires, laxity of morals made the relationship of the various children in the nurseries rather confusing but, although they were left for the most part to the attentions of governesses and servants, filial affection was very strong.

The most welcome result of the better understanding of children's needs was in less physical restraint, and more movement necessitated more comfortable clothes. It was only one small son of a most enlightened parent who was lucky enough to wear loose trousers as early as 1760, for the fashion of putting a boy straight away into grown-up breeches as soon as he left off baby skirts continued until the late 1770's. This new innovation gave the fashion a label, as the intermediate stage between boyhood and manhood, and no doubt it was as readily discarded as it had been eagerly welcomed. Boys' trousers were based on the loose slacks worn by sailors and countrymen and had slits at the ankle for even greater freedom. The waist could be high over a loose shirt, or a more grown-up waistcoat could be worn. The hiatus usual in the reluctant meeting of small boys' garments was sometimes covered by a wide sash or cummerbund. Coats were slim, short and cut away, all now with collars and lapels, but the most typical of details was the wide open, turned-back shirt collar. The urge towards freedom of ideas has always tended to go to a man's neck and in these boys' collars we see how Rousseau's doctrine was now bearing fruit – an early sign of the romantic upsurge that was to become personified in the dress of our later poets. The fashion felt to be so touching and soulful has been the burden of quite normal little boys ever since, through the time of 'Bubbles' up to the bridal pages of to-day.

The manservant in our picture, carrying the schoolboy's inevitable tuck-box, has obviously brought his young master home for the holidays. He wears the high-collared coat that came in with the late 1780's, on which the cuffs have become mere buttoned bands. His waistcoat, too, has lapels and collar, and the neck-cloth shows the beginning of the high and loosely wound style that reached extremes ten years later. The English hat had lost the three-cornered cock that had been the fashion for so long, and became the basis of a style that lasted almost throughout the next century.

The new freedom released little girls from early tight lacing into corsets. It was in women's dress that the back-to-nature and the new classical ideal could best be shown. Fussy frills, festoons and padding disappeared (except for those lacking natural curves) and girls' dresses soon followed the simple flowing line, with a more comfortable bodice and an attached skirt. The soft muslin of which they were mostly made, in light colours or with dainty sprig patterns, was sufficiently full to dispense with innumerable petticoats, and although it was many a day before even a little girl's legs could be shown, skirts were shorter and could be girded up for boisterous games.

It was not only in dress that the small girl still reflected the costume of her mother. Large mob caps now crowned the wider and looser spread of woman's hairdressing and for out-of-doors huge floppy hats, sometimes with a cavalier air or like large lampshades, now covered all, but could look equally charming on a girl's natural undressed curls.

c. 1780   c. 1780   1780   1787   c. 1780

Children's and Manservant's Dress

PLATE XVIII

Fashionable Dress

1777–1780

The Rococo style in art was played out by the 1770's and its freakish ornament had become self-conscious and degenerate. The back-to-nature call of the philosophers posed a knotty problem for designers still caught up in the cupids and volutes of the most fussily decorated period in history. The only answer was a return to a more severe and primitive form of art, of which at that time the lately discovered classical ruins of Pompeii and Sicily were the handiest examples. It was a fortunate choice as the artists and designers had a fund of good taste to draw upon – the later overdone ornamentation of Rome having mercifully disintegrated.

The architects had the first innings by straightening up the fundamental lines into graceful columns and reducing the twiddles and curves of applied ornament to logical forms. Swags of flowers, attached at the ends, took the place of wildly rioting decoration applied indiscriminately. Interiors became more stately but lost a great deal of intimacy and charm. On the whole a very satisfactory compromise was reached by converting severe classicism into pretty elegance. It was the dress designers who took rather a long time to meet the challenge, and we see frills, ruching and bouncy fashions looking rather out of place in their new frigid background. It took a revolution to make woman abandon her padding and reveal the shape of her head as nature intended.

Social behaviour, too, was at the crossroads, restless but undecided as to its next direction. In the meantime life was geared up to its greatest velocity in the pursuit of pleasure and the provision of the means of constant amusement. Vast fortunes were spent in England (where they could be afforded by such people as the Duke of Devonshire with an income of £125,000 a year) on grandiose building and entertainment, which in many ways was to the advantage of local industry and the betterment of agricultural estates. This was a contrast to the situation in France where estates were drained to provide the means of high living for the now nearly always absent owners. Vast fortunes were also frittered on the mania for gambling in both countries, an occupation that was provided for in every place of entertainment.

The English public pleasure gardens of Vauxhall and Ranelagh had proved such a success that even the French were led to imitate them, with provision for both indoor and outdoor entertainment, in the form of fireworks, spectacles and dancing, with, of course, the inevitable gaming rooms. Those of the French aristocracy still with money to burn had their private pleasure gardens, but only those of the truest blue blood were invited. The tedium of always meeting the same faces and the strain of thinking up new diversions tempted them to sneak off and join in the fun – strictly incognito – at the public pleasure gardens where the otherwise despised *bourgeoisie* took relaxation. The opportunity for showmanship and the temptation of fortune-making prompted a few sharp but shady characters to engage in public entertainment on the grand scale. It was received with much favour in England by those less gifted with ideas or unwilling to meet the cost of such lavish private hospitality, and establishments were run, under the sponsorship of great names and by public subscription, by enterprising professional hostesses. The sparkle of the fireworks and the taste of the suppers arranged by the famous Mrs Cornelys at Carlisle House are legends to this day. All this excitement is apparent in the clothes, which reached a peak of flamboyance very different from the well-balanced grace of the early Rococo costume.

A rebellion against austerity by young men unwilling to sink into the obscurity of plain English clothes had started earlier in the century. By the 1770's the exploits of these Macaronis (from the Italian term meaning mix-up or fantasy) equalled in publicity and stupidity the efforts of any modern group. It was they who outdid the height of feminine hairdressing and perched tiny hats on top and were the first to allow their cutaway coats to have long tails. Their fantastic clothes were the last serious revolt against practical dress for men, for although the

French perpetrated further nonsense during the last years of the century the Englishman became buttoned up in his sensible cloth coat for ever. The 'back-to-nature' cry from Rousseau and the practical Dr Tronchin had rather a lame response from their luxury-loving contemporaries but a few ventured on the advice to nurse their own babies, do a little gardening and take walks. This last had the effect of shortening women's skirts, and as the transition to a fully designed short skirt would have been too severe, the previous long dresses became looped up to give the air of lightness and suitability. The short panniers enlarging hips and rear were slightly reduced in size and underskirts were looped in festoons on to stiff petticoats. The upper part of the dress is the most typical of the period being the old *robe à la française* in a new disguise. The over-dress or coat-dress with, in its early stages, the pleats at the back left free, was caught up in two places at the back by cords and tassels to form three long festoons over the underskirt and took the name of the *polonaise*. Later models had the backs seamed and fitted close to the figure but the sections were cut all in one piece from shoulder to hem. Frilled ruching finished the edges and the front closed at the waist with the corsage trimmed with the usual bows. The now popular little jacket, the caraco, was rather a different garment, though with longer skirts treated in the same way it took the name of the caraco *à la polonaise*. This garment, with variations of tails and basques, was the typical feminine mode of the next decade and the forerunner of our walking and tailored suits.

The next step in tune with the classical fervour was in the abandonment of wide hip pads and the adoption of the straight hanging skirt. Not until the next decade was woman persuaded to leave off her frills, and her *polonaise* was still bunched in a perky bustle at the back, but a slight indication of a new line can be seen in the folded bertha collar pouching over the bosom.

Hairdressing, which reached its ultimate height by 1777, gradually widened at the top, was looser and had the back piece turned under in a bag or clubbed shape, with or without roll curls hanging on the neck. Bonnets now covered the top of the hair and eventually enveloped it. The clutter of long sticks, fans, fobs and châtelaines are the obvious signs of an artificial mincing mode that was on the way out.

The main change in men's clothes was in the increasing backward sweep of the coat into swallow tails and the now almost general adoption of the wide-brimmed hat that was beginning to be blocked into a form. Stockings made on the new machines now showed ribbing.

The re-introduction of the large muff was a fashion for women that was to last for several decades, and hints at a return to severe winters.

c. 1780

c. 1777

c. 1780

Fashionable Dress

PLATE XIX

Fashionable Dress

The late 18th century was a golden age for Britain. Greater prosperity was more widely distributed and as yet the great game of making money for itself had not completely overwhelmed certain members of the community as it did in the 19th century. Some of the greatest fortunes had admittedly been made by the foul means of slavery but its beastlier aspects were far removed from these pleasant isles and other rich possessions had come by easier and fairer means. The loss of the American colonies was a nasty jar but the navy still ruled the waves and the country was still practically self-supporting. If we draw a veil over the foul prison conditions and the inadequate Poor Law, as did the more fortunate members of society, the picture looks very pleasant. Peace and a certain amount of civil liberty made for a relaxed society, a great number of whom (from some inborn streak of character) used the prosperity for ends other than ostentation and the ceaseless pursuit of frivolous pleasure. This complacency and restraint is apparent in all the arts of the period. There was little rushing after the novel or contrary as society knew exactly what it wanted and the artists and craftsmen were in tune with their patrons. The greatest wealth was still in the hands of the aristocracy but the professional and cultured middle class all influenced the standard of production by the quality of their demands. Better roads and superb English carriages started the travel fever that enlarged experience and filled our country houses with the not-specially-manufactured souvenirs of other countries. These early journeys, being no package tours, afforded time and opportunity to absorb the great periods of European art, and, as they in their turn had nothing tawdry or worthless to offer, the knowledge gained only heightened an already critical and selective taste. What distinguished the English culture in contrast to that of other European countries was its fundamentally utilitarian character. The furniture, especially, was made for use and comfort, not merely for decoration or filling a space in a room. Architecture, even of the great houses, was not pretentious and followed rational rules of proportion that were understood and used by even the humblest builder. The manufacturer was still the craftsman and, not being called upon to cater for a wholesale market, could devote his time to producing the high quality demanded by the customer of good taste.

The most felicitous aspect of this situation was that people had not yet seen anything really bad and the common man was satisfied with articles of the same craftsmanship, but of simpler form than those of the wealthy customer. The same assurance applied also to costume. The slightly strained relations with France, during the wars in India, Canada and America, had rather thrown the people back on their own resources in the way of fashion, although the intrepid travellers still passed through that country and brought back hints of what was being worn in the highest circles across the Channel. What is more, they were also seen by the French, and the simple, comely, comfortable clothes the English had evolved for themselves became the rage with the French *beau-monde* who were getting heartily tired of their frills and furbelows. Simplicity became the keynote for clothes and behaviour, with Marie-Antoinette leading the charade in a milkmaid's dress at her little farm at Versailles.

The passion for sport had already overwhelmed the British male and his clothes were the outcome of all the driving, riding, boxing and gymnastics in which every fit young man participated. Coats, already tight, now only fastened across the chest and were well cut away to give ease in riding and to show a manly torso. Breeches were lengthened at the knees to meet the tops of boots which, for the same reason, became the fashion again. Collars rose, either as a band or a wide turn-over, up to the ears, and the lapels of the waistcoat poked out either side of the chin. Hats were now blocked into many sporting shapes: the coachman, the postillion and even a few embryo top hats with wide or narrower curling brims. The French version of 'du sporting' was a little odd, in fact a caricature of the Englishman's passion as he was less accustomed to an outdoor life and, taking the stable into the drawing-room, so to speak, dolled it up in quite unsuitable materials. Every detail was exaggerated, with coat-tails longer and waists shorter and the already high stock becoming ear- and chin-enveloping. The most evocative detail of the period is the striped pattern material that we know in this country as the Regency stripe, but which was undoubtedly a French inspiration that evolved from the design of materials popular through several decades. The typical brocades of the Rococo period were woven in stripes with an alternate band of flowers in serpentine patterns. When the more decorated costumes and materials were abandoned in favour of a sprucer style the stripe, alone, was retained to accent the longer sweep and sharper angles of the new clothes. The Frenchman was delighted with the fantastic effect, and although he may have been inspired in the first place by the stockings worn by our Macaronis, he used the stripe more for costume than the English, who preferred it for interior decoration.

The change in women's clothes was apparent, much earlier, when the Englishwoman left off her bunched bustle and ruched trimmings and allowed her skirt to sweep back in an unbroken line from waist to hem. This was yet another outcome of the sporting trend as her riding-habit had followed this line for some time past and was found to be very much more dignified than the short and perky previous fashion. The long tight sleeves were probably derived from the same source and gave the wearer the look of sleek tailor-made assurance that matched that of the male. For this was also a more rosy age for woman, if not entirely golden. Even the women victims of the Revolution met death with a dignity born of self-reliance, and the Englishwoman had a much freer life in sport and travel and a share in the great game of politics. Not only a Duchess of Devonshire, offering a kiss for every vote for the Whigs, but the talent and behaviour of great actresses made them accepted in the highest society and gave them greater independence. The enterprising Mrs Abingdon, of Drury Lane Theatre, was not only admired but drew a fat income, on the side, from the most respectable occupation of giving advice on the fashions to those less smart or experienced.

With a simple line of skirt all the interest of the toilette could be concentrated on the hat. As hairdressing widened, bonnets had become larger to enclose the top. With still looser hair the bonnets were then wired and trimmed into fantastic lampshade hats out of which grew the real hat shapes loaded with bows, feathers and flowers. The great English hats had a dual inspiration : sport, and the romantic trend that brought back the Stuart collars at the same time. Many of them had crowns blocked into square or sugar-loaf shapes, and what set the English style apart was that the trimming, however extravagant, never obscured the shape of the crown.

The still long bodice sank into the gathered folds of the skirt at the waist, a small pad lifted the back of the skirt in a rounded sweep, and another symbol of the period finished the neck : the English woman's dearly beloved kerchief now came into its own as never before; in fine gauze, widened and pouched high over the bosom, it was sometimes crossed over and tied at the back, or was tucked into the corsage in front to emphasize the long tight waist.

Both men and women now wore the hair loose and full, turned under into a large roll with, in the case of the women, curls falling below on the neck.

It is astonishing how quickly a new fashion had spread to all classes of the community even before the time of machine-made clothes. If Wheatley's *Cries of London* are at all truthful the women of the poorer classes had grasped the essentials of the new line, had pouched their kerchiefs and donned large hats before 1794.